FORESIGHT

JOHN SANEI

DEDICATION

To Sean Mckenna, Paul Jeffries, Mark Sham and
Ilan Green, my brothers from another mother,
and the critical sounding boards who help me do
my best, most vulnerable thinking. Thank you – your
huge hearts and wise minds mean the world to me.

FORESIGHT

AWAKEN CURIOSITY.
CULTIVATE WISDOM.
DISCOVER THE
ABUNDANT FUTURE

JOHN SANEI

'John Sanei's genius is in helping us decode and overcome the obstacles we face in achieving personal and professional success.'
– Nadia Bilchik, CNN

'The end of the old way is not doomsday. It's a climb up a new mountain. And when you think like John thinks, it's a beautiful climb.'
– Cal Fussman, *New York Times* bestselling author

'John Sanei is a local trailblazer with a global understanding of the changes the world's businesses and economies are going through.'
– Autodesk

'Thanks for rocking our sales conference.'
– Thomson Reuters UAE

'John's frank honesty, militant optimism and abundance thinking are liberating to any audience. He never fails to enthuse and inspire – and his ideas are worth listening to!'
– Exxaro

JOHN

'John Sanei encourages new
ways of thinking. As a speaker,
he's definitely worth having
on the line-up.'
– Dubizzle, UAE

'Incredible insights...
inspirational.'
– Dell SA

'Very few people can
command the attention
of a room like John Sanei.
He is a magnetic presenter.
Quite simply, he does not
settle for mediocrity –
and it shows.'
– Meltwater

'Mind blown.'
– Alan Winde,
Western Cape Premier

SANEI

Published by Mercury
an imprint of Burnet Media

•

Burnet Media is the publisher of Mercury, Two Dogs and Two Pups books
info@burnetmedia.co.za   www.burnetmedia.co.za
PO Box 53557, Kenilworth, 7745, South Africa

•

First published 2019
1 3 5 7 9 8 6 4 2

•

Publication © 2019 Burnet Media
Text © 2019 John Sanei
Cover and interior author portraits © Guido Schwarz Photography
Other imagery © Pexels, Unsplash, Shutterstock

•

•

Distributed by Jacana Media
www.jacana.co.za

•

Printed and bound by Tandym Print
www.tandym.co.za

•

ISBN 9781928230748
Also available in ebook and audiobook

Set in PMN Caecilia 9.5pt

ABOUT THE AUTHOR

John Sanei is an author, speaker and trend specialist fascinated with what it takes to activate the FOREsight needed to create an abundant future.

His goal in life is to bring courage, clarity, elegance and consciousness to audiences around the world, a mission that sees him travelling regularly from his bases in Cape Town and Dubai to work with global brands and governments.

He explores human psychology, business strategies and future studies in his workshops, presentations and best-selling books.

John was Africa's first Singularity University faculty member, and is a lecturer at Duke Corporate University. He was chosen as *GQ* South Africa's most influential and connected man of 2018.

His previous books are *What's Your Moonshot?* and *Magnetiize*, and in 2019 he was invited to contribute to *Future Shock At 50*, a collection of essays by the world's top 100 futurists.

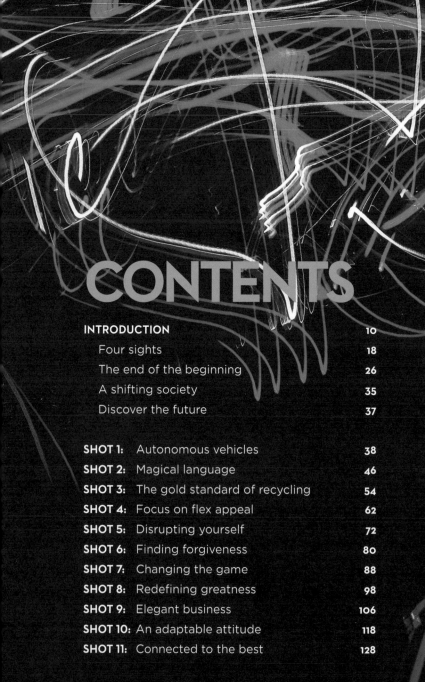

CONTENTS

INTRODUCTION 10
Four sights 18
The end of the beginning 26
A shifting society 35
Discover the future 37

SHOT 1: Autonomous vehicles 38
SHOT 2: Magical language 46
SHOT 3: The gold standard of recycling 54
SHOT 4: Focus on flex appeal 62
SHOT 5: Disrupting yourself 72
SHOT 6: Finding forgiveness 80
SHOT 7: Changing the game 88
SHOT 8: Redefining greatness 98
SHOT 9: Elegant business 106
SHOT 10: An adaptable attitude 118
SHOT 11: Connected to the best 128

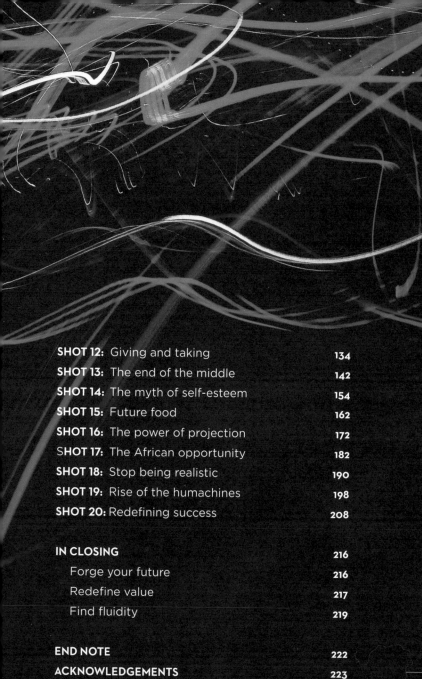

SHOT 12: Giving and taking — 134

SHOT 13: The end of the middle — 142

SHOT 14: The myth of self-esteem — 154

SHOT 15: Future food — 162

SHOT 16: The power of projection — 172

S**HOT 17:** The African opportunity — 182

SHOT 18: Stop being realistic — 190

SHOT 19: Rise of the humachines — 198

SHOT 20: Redefining success — 208

IN CLOSING — 216

Forge your future — 216

Redefine value — 217

Find fluidity — 219

END NOTE — 222

ACKNOWLEDGEMENTS — 223

INTRODUCTION

I was a naughty kid back in the day. Not because I disrespected my mom or hated listening, but because – I'd like to think – I was busy connecting invisible dots.

It started when I was about five or six years old and I really, *really* wanted a new pair of Nike trainers. They were expensive: too much for a single mom, and I knew it. So instead of asking her for the shoes outright, I convinced her I needed them for a fictitious tennis match.

Eventually she caved and, man, was I stoked with those Nikes.

For several days I figured I was in the clear... until she asked my friends how the match had gone. When all they could do was look confused, the game was up, and I had a few well-deserved slippers flung my way.

I pulled a similar stunt at the OK Bazaar in the town of Middleburg a few years later, this time to get my feet into a new pair of Reeboks. When no-one was looking, I swapped price tags with a far cheaper pair of North Stars, and my mom became my unwitting accomplice when she agreed to buy them. Sorry, Mamman.

On the surface these stories may seem like a kid just messing around, or perhaps the start of a disconcerting sneaker fetish, but I've come to understand them as the first glimpses into a deeper part of my identity.

Nike wasn't a powerhouse brand when I suddenly 'took up' tennis. Michael Jordan hadn't sunk his first pro basket yet, let alone launched the Air Jordan. But something inside me connected a pair of shoes on a shelf to a billion-dollar business that was still finding its feet. Then, with the arrival of Reebok on the scene, a part of me sensed the great shoe-brand rivalry that would follow. (It's fair to say Nike went on to win that one.)

I felt the same connection the first time I saw Acupuncture Footwear in Shelley's Covent Garden in London. It was 1997, and they were the first dress-up/dress-down trainers, meaning you could wear them with shorts or a suit. Radical.

This was BG (Before Google), so I had to let my fingers do the talking and find the owner of the brand in the phone book. It took me nearly three months, but I eventually tracked him down and set up a meeting.

I bought some second-hand clothes in Camden so I could suit up and, at age 23, managed to secure my first distribution agency. I got the shoes into 40 boutiques back in South Africa, as well as Edgars, a major player back then. I then used the money I made to buy my first restaurant.

I made the move from footwear to food because I had that same sense of excitement the first time I sat in a Primi Piatti restaurant in 1999. I could just tell they would be huge. I went on to own five Primis by 2008 – a story you'll know well if you've read my previous books.

It kept happening. Also in 1999 I tried to bring G-Star clothing to South Africa before it became a truly iconic label. In 2008 I secured the rights to import Chromagen solar water heaters from Israel – just in time for the countrywide blackouts that started that year. There are other stories like this, but I'd like to write more books, so I'll leave it there for now.

Point is, I wouldn't have been able to tell you how or why I knew these opportunities had potential at the time, but it turns out that I had a knack for spotting consumer expectations and the trends that address them. Where others didn't even know the dots existed, I found myself connecting them, from early opportunity through to long-term brand success.

SEEING THE INVISIBLE

I believe we all have the ability to see the invisible in some aspects of our lives – and it's always amazing to see the process in action.

I'm talking about the comedian who can find something to laugh about even in the most mundane moments. The architect who looks at an empty piece of ground and conjures up an incredible house. The interior designer who makes that stack of bricks a home. My girlfriend, a genius hairstylist who will give you the best cut you never knew you needed. My mom, flinger of slippers, mother of a sneaker swindler, who can transform mere soil and seeds into a gorgeous garden.

These qualities are more than just small talk at parties. They are the gifts that energise, excite and define us. And once we understand how they work, develop our ability to use them and share them with others, we can redefine our own perspective and connect the invisible dots between the possible and the real.

THAT'S WHAT THIS BOOK IS ALL ABOUT: THE ANTICIPATION OF CHANGE USING OUR OWN GENIUS.

My intention in these pages is to share 20 SHOTs of FOREsight that I hope will offer you a window into the future and propel you through it with ease and abundance.

CERTAINTY VS FREEDOM

Before we can explore FOREsight, though, we need to understand how most people see the world.

For centuries, most of the Western World favoured certainty over freedom – whether they wanted to or not. Governed by religion and the society around them, people knew they would live according to a strict set of rules. And that still happens in parts of the world today. Many Mediterranean villages offer prime examples.

Consider the island of Sicily. The average small Sicilian town of 2,000 people provides its inhabitants with 15 churches to attend. That's a 1:133 church-to-person ratio. The church sets the tempo for every aspect of life, and from a young age residents know who they are, how they fit into their community, what their duties and obligations are, who they're likely to marry, where they're going to live, work and die, and how to cope with pain and suffering.

Their lives are secure, with a large degree of certainty. But there's not much freedom.

Through much of the world, though, certainty has gone a little stale. We don't like being told what to do, so we've replaced rules with choices. Now we choose where we live, how we live, what work we do, whether to have kids, what we eat, when we wake up, what colour finish we want on our new phone, whether to swipe left or right...

We rightly celebrate freedom, but in unlocking its power we find ourselves facing endless options. To borrow from French existentialist Jean-Paul Sartre, the freedom to make decisions and the responsibility for every decision you make are an enormous and intimidating burden. And in the increasingly fluid and hyperconnected world of today, we are faced with far more decisions on a daily basis than Jean-Paul ever was.

In swapping security and certainty for choice and freedom – as integral as it is to modern identity – we find that we've unlocked a state of perpetual anxiety, which is increasingly exacerbated by our position on the cusp of a new era in humankind.

WE FIND OURSELVES TRYING TO MAKE INFORMED DECISIONS ABOUT A TOMORROW THAT'S NEAR-IMPOSSIBLE TO PREDICT.

WISDOM + CURIOSITY = FLOW STATE

When we try to make difficult decisions, the natural impulse is to look around – and backwards – to absorb as much information as we can to find the solution. It's instinctive.

To thrive today, however, and to connect our own invisible dots to success, we need to look forward into the future, not with fear and trepidation but with wisdom and curiosity.

Twentieth-century philosopher Alan Watts said that to be knowledgeable, a man must learn something new every day, but to be wise he must *unlearn* something new each day – and that's never been truer than in the modern data-deluged world. To cultivate the type of open-minded wisdom we need today, we must let go of the prejudices and ingrained ideas that blur our vision for tomorrow.

Then we have to get curious. When we start asking questions, we move through the world with an excitement and flexibility that makes today's impossible, tomorrow's goal. Curious people thought: what is the moon, where is the moon, how can we *get* to the moon?

Curiosity compels you to follow your heart and draw the excitement from every moment of every day.

'We keep moving forward, opening new doors and doing new things, because we're curious and curiosity keeps leading us down new paths.'

WALT DISNEY, entrepreneur, animator and film producer

Combining the chemicals of wisdom and curiosity in the right way results in an unstoppable chain reaction that powers you towards the much sought-after *flow* state. In this state, time takes on a new meaning as it becomes almost malleable, and your whole temporal perspective shifts. You are inspired to create and invent. You prioritise flexibility and adaptability. And you experience energy that doesn't fade.

When you intentionally strive for wisdom and live a curious life, you adjust the lens that you use to peer into the future. And you find yourself more and more able to connect the invisible dots that you need to move from possibility to reality.

‖‖‖ ‖‖‖‖

SUMMARY 1

Our society has discarded security and certainty in favour of abundant choice. As magnificent as this can be, it is an increasingly heavy burden to bear – one that blurs our vision of tomorrow.

We need to break our habit of looking to the past for answers; we must strive for wisdom by unlearning what we think we know; and we must become curious about today's world. In doing so we are more likely to reach the flow state, where true productivity and fulfilment lie.

FOUR SIGHTS

Seeing is what happens when you open your eyes, right? Not necessarily.

The future is happening right now, and how we perceive it is paramount in how we prepare for it. I've come to realise that we use four distinct types of sight: what I call HINDsight, PLAINsight, INsight and FOREsight. And it's critical we get to grips with each of them to ready our perspective for the hyperconnected future that awaits us.

HINDSIGHT: Made from memories

There's a dangerous idiom that's been on the loose for a while now: 'Hindsight is 20:20.' It seems an innocent enough idea, and when we think, 'I should have done this instead of that', it make sense. But it carries with it an inherent danger: second-guessing every choice you make because of how it looks in retrospect won't help you confront the future. That's a pathway to regret and little else.

HINDsight isn't really seeing at all. It's what happens when we apply memory to our current situation, and use that to figure out our next move. But ideas that were innovative and bold yesterday just might not hold up today or tomorrow or the day after in an exponentially changing world.

Think of it as trying to remember how to tango – except the DJ is now playing the latest Billboard Number 1.

HINDsight does have its uses – when you're operating in old systems, for instance – but relying on a familiar past is only ever going to give you predictable ideas, which are of ever-diminishing value in our illogical future.

PLAINSIGHT: Physical perception

PLAINsight is what happens when you open your eyes. It's vital to get us through the day, and allows us to tango without bumping into other couples, but it has enormous limits when it comes to developing a future-ready perspective.

The biggest shortcoming of PLAINsight is that, as writer Anaïs Nin observed, 'We don't see things as they are, but as we are.' Sounds like a throwaway Instagram caption, but it's true: we are subjective beings, and our experiences, prejudices and circumstances shape the way we interpret the world. That means we're never getting the full picture, regardless of how objective we're trying to be.

What we see with our eyes is processed through three filters, and it's helpful to understand them so that we are better able to adapt to the future, to become future-fluid.

The first filter is our identity – who we are, where we come from and how we fit into this world. Our identity, whether individual, group or a combination thereof, dictates our perspective on everything. (Group identity has, with some reason, gained increasing notoriety in the age of identity politics; its effect is widespread.)

The second filter is our emotions. How we feel when we perceive something affects the *way* we perceive it. The corollary is that when we recall those perceptions we may trigger the same emotions. So, for instance, it becomes difficult to hold a measured view on a bad breakup or a work failure when your recollections of those events are associated with anger and resentment. It's up to us to choose whether to blame or thank the past for the memories it's given us – a choice I wrote about in *What's Your Moonshot?*

The third and last filter is our primal state. This is all about the reptilian brain, hardwired for survival, which influences our every interaction. It's our instinctive fight-or-flight trigger, and it's evident when we choose to run away from problems or towards opportunity.

Each of these factors affects the way we process and perceive the world around us, and project our personality onto our perspective. As renowned contemporary thinker Dr Joe Dispenza puts it, 'Our personality creates our personal reality.'

A single perspective can never be the whole truth, and it's a pity – tragic, even – that those who become mired in PLAINsight believe it to be the case. They overlook the factors behind the things they see, and as a result ignore the faith, intuition and hope that they need to future-proof themselves.

INSIGHT: Where information becomes ideas

INsight is the realisation that there are loads of other dances besides the tango – but never trying to learn any of them.

Most of us, myself included, have had that Sunday-night epiphany when we realise we need to make some sort of change. We commit to living a new life of resolve and motivation... until midway through Monday morning when we realise we have to actually do something.

People who rely on INsight are academically rich. They have all the knowledge – they've read the books, seen the speakers, listened to the podcasts – and yet they cannot change because they've never learnt to apply what they learn. I know this space well, because I used to be there.

The American futurist Herman Kahn called it 'the Expert Problem'. The Western way of learning teaches us how to think within specific frameworks and systems, but the more 'educated' we become, the less able we are to recognise solutions that don't fall into the frameworks we've been taught. We study, but we don't live what we learn – so we never make true progress.

To change this perspective, you need to understand the reason behind your inaction, and ask yourself a big question:

'Is the idea of change causing pain, or is my inability to change causing pain?'

'One reason people resist change is because they focus on what they have to give up, instead of what they have to gain.'

RICK GODWIN, pastor and author

It took me a long time to understand that change is only as exciting or frightening as we want it to be, and to actually apply what I'd learnt along the road. But when it all clicked, and I understood that I had been scared simply because I thought I couldn't do it, my perspective completely changed, and I started to actively live the knowledge I'd accumulated.

People with INsight might realise that they need to adapt for the future, but they are unable to act on that understanding. To do so, they need to take the step to FOREsight.

FORESIGHT: Connecting the invisible dots

I'm sure you know the feeling of staring at a client brief, a business proposal or a half-filled crossword puzzle with no idea what to do next. Then... something happens. You pause. You gather your thoughts. Then somehow you transcend the hamster-wheel pattern of thinking that's been getting you nowhere and inspiration strikes.

> THAT MOMENT OF BLINDING CLARITY
> THAT ALLOWS YOU TO SOLVE A PROBLEM
> WITH AN ELEGANT SOLUTION?
> THAT'S FORESIGHT!

FOREsight is the magic that allows us to ride the rainbow to the pot of gold at the end – and to get there, we need to understand and evolve through the other perspectives.

We need to awaken our curiosity and cultivate our wisdom so that they become the default way we engage with the world; this way we will start recognising patterns and opportunities we wouldn't if we were relying on memory (HINDsight), perception (PLAINsight) or information (INsight) alone.

Throughout these pages, I talk about our 'genius', that element that I believe exists in each of us to connect invisible dots. We are all geniuses on some level. In the case of Albert Einstein, he was a literal genius, so I find it appropriate that, in one simple quote, he nailed the difference between HINDsight, PLAINsight and INsight on one side and FOREsight on the other (incorporating my understanding of wisdom in the process):

'A clever person solves a problem.
A wise person avoids it.'
ALBERT EINSTEIN, genius

To return to the tango one last time, FOREsight is the moment when you realise there are hundreds of other dances, and that you have what you need to learn them all and express yourself through dance.

With FOREsight, the future is fluid and exciting, not stagnant and scary.

With FOREsight, you can be optimistic and excited to experiment.

With FOREsight, your head and heart are given the freedom to act with today in mind, tomorrow in preparation, and the day after that in excitement.

IIIIIIIIIIIIIIIIIIIIIIIIIIIIIIIIIIIIIIIIIIIIIIIIIIIIIIIIIIIIIIIIIIIIIIIIIIII IIII

SUMMARY 2

To make the right choices in our modern world of endless options, we must understand our perspective on the world, which means understanding the four types of sight.

HINDsight is about looking back; which helps less and less in a constantly changing future. PLAINsight is reliant on physical perception, which is inherently limiting and can cut us off from countless forces of inspiration. INsight is the academic knowledge that lacks the heart and conviction needed to actually get things done.

We find that heart and conviction in FOREsight, which allows us to act on the knowledge we have with energy and excitement, and the understanding that structure is essential for connecting the invisible dots between today and tomorrow – and the day after and the week after and the year after...

THE END OF
THE BEGINNING

Imagine taking a trip back to 1999, when Britney Spears was top of the charts with ...*Baby One More Time* and *The Sixth Sense* was freaking everyone out, and telling people about the future today. How we buy our groceries online, and send pictures of what we're eating to our friends, and use our phones to try on makeup, and get our refrigerators to write our shopping lists. You'd be met with blank stares.

Two decades later, this is our reality. Today we have an internet infrastructure that connects half the world's population, with the other four billion set to come online in the near future.

Mass connectivity means more than an overload of *Candy Crush* players and potential traffic to your website. It's more than a business opportunity: it's fundamentally changing the way our world works. It's the wheel or the printing press or the electricity of our time.

As a result, it's making people afraid – but this is a fear we've faced before.

On your trip back to 1999, when people asked about the future, you'd have to assure them that the world wasn't about to descend into chaos when the date clicked over to 2000. Back then, Y2K paranoia had everyone worried about aeroplanes falling out of the sky and stock markets spinning out of control because our archaic computers supposedly couldn't handle the 19-20 date rollover. It was a panic roughly on par with the postman's reaction when he first saw a fax machine, or your local phone-line company when briefcase-sized cellphones started arriving in stores.

Looking back, the level of anxiety around these technological watersheds seems ridiculous, yet here we are again. Artificial intelligence, machine learning, cryptocurrencies and bioengineering – these are the trigger words that fuel the fears of contemporary society, because we don't recognise we're reliving a pattern of development we've seen before. The difference now is that everything is just happening much faster; several game-changing technologies are evolving at a rapid pace, and there's too much data for us to process to be able to keep up with it all.

Anxiety will always be present when we change the present faster than we're comfortable with, but I believe the best way to overcome our anxiety is to teach ourselves to be excited and energised by change. As I see it, we're at the end of the beginning of the innovation age. Our near future will be driven by four key technologies, and we need to get to know them so we can best engage in that future.

INFO TECH

Information technology refers to devices that we will wear, swallow, smell and look at to collect as much data as possible about ourselves, our bodies and our world.

Sound creepy? Chances are you're already the proud owner of a smartwatch that can track your basic health indicators. If you are, you're one of millions around the world, and thus invested in info tech. (As of 2017, Apple was the world's largest watch manufacturer, with 15 million sales a year and revenues exceeding those of Rolex.)

But it's not just about counting your steps, tracking your sleep patterns or measuring your mood (or that of your partner). From jackets that regulate your temperature to combining your digital and physical world by using Magic Leap One goggles[1], this space is about finding ways to make us live better, healthier and happier.

The sector is currently being fuelled by the introduction of two game-changing tech upgrades:

☐ 5G, the next generation of mobile internet connectivity. This will give us a more stable, faster online mobile experience, with global roll-out expected in 2020.

☐ Internet Protocol 6, the updated communication system that directs online traffic. Whereas IP4, the previous incarnation, could connect about 4.3 billion devices, IP6, being phased in in parallel with IP4, will be able to connect so many devices you can't count that high (technically around 340 duodecillion).

The implication of this double upgrade is comprehensive access, both fixed and mobile, to unlimited information and interconnectivity. We can pretty much connect anyone and anything to anyone and anything.

INsights, anyone?

MACHINE LEARNING

Machine learning is the artificial intelligence that allows machines to perform tasks more effectively with practice, rather than being programmed to do them in a specific way from the start.

You see this every time Google offers you suggestions to complete your search requests. The 'machine' has 'learnt' what you're most likely to be looking for based on the way you browse the internet. Similarly, music and content-streaming services such as Spotify and Netflix learn your preferences the more you use them, and in time can make suggestions that are often superior to your own, chiefly because machines have an exponentially larger selection to choose from (an entire database versus our shoddy human memory).

Put another way, machine learning programming categorises and contextualises data that technology provides. In an age when we are overwhelmed with data, identifying the important bits is only going to become more and more important.

Once that information is placed into the correct framework, we can start using it to live more intelligent, seamless, abundant lives in which absolutely everything is hyperpersonalised. Our devices will be able to recommend what we should eat, how we should exercise, what to study, *if* we should study, what job to pursue, who to date – every aspect of our life will be informed by the application of intelligent data custom-designed for each of us. (Yes, this is a good thing!)

BIO TECH

The essence of life is being digitised, and we're moving away from medical technology towards biological technology. Ultimately we want to prevent problems rather than having to solve them. (Einstein would approve.) This is the space where we use information, software and hardware to augment human health and wellbeing.

Pretty soon, perfectly healthy babies with super-human eyesight will become the new normal. Travellers will be able to swallow a pill at take-off to monitor their wellbeing during a flight. We will be able to buy a peach packed with 100g of protein that tastes like a watermelon. By applying the CRISPR-Cas9 genome-editing tool – technology that allows geneticists and medical researchers to 'edit' parts of the genome by removing, adding or altering sections of the DNA sequence – we will be able to combine, redesign and reinvent life at a genetic level, and create whatever we choose.

The net result for humanity will be longer, richer, healthier lives – not forgetting that we are already the longest-living, richest and healthiest humans to have walked the planet.

BLOCKCHAIN

Blockchain is a digital verification system that securely stores information shared across a network of decentralised computers. Put another way, blockchain provides an infallible record of what has happened.

While it has found global notoriety as the technology behind cryptocurrencies like Bitcoin and Ethereum, blockchain's potential applications go far beyond market speculation. It has the potential to change everything from financial management to the way we vote to how we trace food supplies – and it isn't actually that complicated.

William Mougayar, author of *The Business Blockchain*, likens it to Google Docs.[2]

In the past, collaborating on a document meant it was written, emailed, edited with comments, emailed back, edited again, resent, and so on until everyone was happy (or too fed up to keep going). Google Docs allows people with permission to work on that document instantly, simultaneously, in front of everyone, online. The efficiencies are exponential.

Right now, blockchain is like the first mobile phones: it's slow and difficult to use, and it feels a bit weird. Not many people truly understand how it works – it's even difficult to predict how much potential it has. But what it lacks in user-friendliness it makes up for with something money can't buy: trust.

Blockchain embeds trust into the DNA of the system you're using. It's transparent, and that strips away the need for lawyers, banks and government institutions – all untrusted entities today. Because it creates a peer-to-peer environment, blockchain says goodbye to the middle man, allowing key transactions to happen in the background so we can live a more seamless life.

A prime example is the taxi industry, which blockchain will develop even further. Experts predict that, in future, you will be able to order an autonomous taxi, which will pull up, recognise your face and greet you by name. You'll hop in and verbally consent to the fare, and hit the road.

That's cool, but it gets better.

If you're running late, you'll be able to politely ask your car to get you to your destination on time. It will ask for more money, which it will then use to pay the cars that are in your way – all connected and blockchain-enabled – to move over.

Safe. Instant. Connected. Convenient. Blockchain is everything our future will be.

These four sectors are already taking businesses and pastimes that don't 'belong' online – like grocery shopping, socialising and cosmetics – and making the brands behind them better decision-makers than we'll ever be.

They are the pillars of the hyperintelligent, hyperpersonalised, hyperefficient, hyperaffordable world we're building. And it's no more daunting than the arrival of the fax machine or the cellphone, as long as you stop thinking innovation and start practising disruption.

> THE DIFFERENCE? INNOVATION IS DOING WHAT YOU'VE ALWAYS DONE BUT MORE EFFICIENTLY. DISRUPTION IS ABOUT CREATING NEW BUSINESS MODELS THAT MAKE THE OLD ONES OBSOLETE.

Brands like Patagonia, SpaceX, Apple and Netflix are using technology to do just that, and appealing to conscious consumers. They've gone beyond selling products to championing and creating a more elegant future. They understand that innovation and disruption have redefined value – and this has elevated them to cult status.

A SHIFTING SOCIETY

We have always understood our value by relating it to our dominant means of production.

When we relied on rain dances and the gods to give us a good harvest, our agricultural society measured value by our relationship with the land.

The Industrial Revolution changed that understanding: rather than praying for abundance, we built machines to produce it. In that production-line reality, we started to understand our place as cogs in the machine, measuring value by how efficiently we performed our role. As Danish economist Keld Holm observed, our society said 'hello to factory rules, assembly-line production, conformity and uniformity for the sake of efficiency'.[3]

The reason the future feels so overwhelming is because we're caught between the mass-production mind-set that measures value according to an industrial index of efficiency, and the inspiring, enlightened world that we can create with new technology. We are moving away from processes and production into a time when ideas and innovation will be what we value most. We're still sleeping off the effects of being part of a machine but we're also *becoming* the machine: Human 2.0, powered by the four pillars of modern technology pushing us to become the best we can be.

Cult brands understand that evolution, and have already set themselves up to meet the needs of the new mankind. Inspired by conscious leaders, they're out to change the world for the future, and they put people and the planet ahead of profit.

Just as the internet has written a new definition for communication, delivery, business, romance and many other everyday concepts, so the emergence of info tech, bio tech, machine learning and blockchain will make reality mean something completely different – for businesses and for you.

SUMMARY 3

Our society is rapidly changing. In the same way our measure of value shifted from agriculture to industry, we're developing a new definition of value, with ideas and innovation at its heart. The new system is being propelled by four key technology pillars: info tech, bio tech, machine learning and blockchain.

The speed of change shouldn't be a cause for fear, because we've faced this kind of disruption before. Instead, we should be excited and ready to embrace opportunity. We need to transform ourselves and our businesses into cult brands: driven by a desire to help humanity live an enlightened life, rather than by a relentless focus on efficiency.

DISCOVER THE FUTURE

The way we perceive tomorrow defines the way we prepare for it. We can be overwhelmed by the unknown, or we can revel in a time of abundant choice – in which case, we have the opportunity to let go of restrictive perspectives, activate our wisdom and curiosity, and start connecting invisible dots towards an exciting and prosperous future.

The power to recognise patterns will allow you to find new opportunities, both in self-development and in business, and to become excited about what you're creating: a future fuelled by your vision.

Each of the 20 SHOTs in the pages ahead offers what I believe is FOREsight into the respective topics they cover. An alternating mix of technology and perspective, they are examples of the unexpected leaps and exponential results that can come from looking and thinking beyond the obvious.

My hope is that in reading them you will not only take with you the specific FOREsight of each SHOT to help prepare you for the future, but also the ability to develop your own FOREsight in your daily life – to allow you to discover the abundant future with courage and optimism.

I encourage you to dissect, discuss and study the 20 SHOTs of FOREsight, and to use them as a toolkit for developing your own.

1

AUTONOMOUS VEHICLES

VEHICLES

HOW DRIVERLESS TRANSPORT
WILL NOT ONLY GET YOU
FROM Ⓐ TO Ⓑ, BUT
CHANGE WHERE
Ⓐ AND Ⓑ ARE

HINDSIGHT

Way back when, our hairy ancestors lived in caves. This was a smart move. Caves offered them a (relatively) dry and warm place to lay their heads at the end of the day, and their odds of surviving the prehistoric predators of the night were that much better than they would have been out in the open.

Over time, we've regularly upgraded our living situation. We learnt how to build shelters in more convenient locations, how to make them secure, then how to farm and create permanent settlements.*

As we incrementally eased the daily struggle for survival, we freed up time for other pursuits, and when the Ancient Egyptians and Mesopotamians unlocked the secrets of mathematics and engineering, they realised it was possible to stack buildings on top of each other and connect them with stairs.

PLAINSIGHT

Stairs were a revelation that changed the world. For thousands of years, we copied the Ancient Egyptian approach, because that's how we'd 'always' done things. Need more space? Stack a few levels and

---

*Possibly because magic mushrooms activated our imagination, as Terence McKenna explains in *Food Of The Gods*[1] – but more on that another time...

connect them with stairs. As our settlements grew, we could save space by going up as well as out and, step by step, stairs shaped the way we lived and worked (often in the same building).

This worked well enough until the dawn of the Industrial Revolution around 1760, at which point our villages started growing into towns and our towns into cities. We needed space for factories and more homes for our expanding urban populations, and we needed to move people ever longer distances between their home and their work. So we created transport networks and the traffic that comes with them.

Industrialised cities grew mostly outwards, with building height limited by the logistical difficulty of getting people and things up and down flights of stairs. To avoid the commute as much as possible, people piled into city centres, raising the value and prices of property close to work. The ground or first floor was hot property, because it meant you didn't need to drag yourself up several flights of stairs after a day spent working yourself to the bone. The poorest of the poor were kicked up to the attic.

Most people didn't realise that this pattern, established over the course of a century or more, was ripe for disruption, probably because they, like many of us today, were stuck in PLAINsight. Buildings couldn't go higher so the city had to keep growing outwards – that was obvious, right?

INSIGHT

Elisha Otis was the man who turned that thinking on its head, and reined in the relentlessly sprawling, tightly compacted three-storey city. In New York in 1852, he thought long and hard, and transformed a handful of existing patents into a brake, creating the world's first autonomous vehicle: the elevator.

Five years later, Otis's first commercial elevator was installed, and we could literally take things to another level, just as the invention of stairs had allowed us to thousands of years earlier.

Now that we could regularly build more than three storeys high, there was plenty more space to be found in the cities – we just had to look up. Otis himself never saw the change he would bring, and it wasn't until 1885 that the world's first 10-storey skyscraper, the Home Insurance Building in Chicago, was opened. Less than 50 years later, the Empire State Building went up, at 102 storeys. The sprouting of high-rise buildings completely changed cityscapes around the world, packing people in sardine-style as they sacrificed space to stay closer to work.

As city living became a reality, prices skyrocketed. The wealthy paid top dollar for penthouses with amazing views a safe distance from the sweaty reality below. The average Joe who couldn't afford to move to the big city was stuck in the suburbs, ferried to his fortune by an overloaded transport network.

The elevator had a more drastic impact on society than stairs had; it even created jobs for the drivers entrusted to get people safely to their floor – and it came about 40 years before the evolution of stairs into the escalator.

FORESIGHT

Otis inadvertently connected the invisible dots between a lifetime of aching legs, ever-sprawling cities and the engineering potential to build really tall buildings. His invention was literally awe-inducing at the time (people gasped) and took decades to have a real effect, and yet it seems so obvious in retrospect (a common measure of FOREsight). He lived during a century of great inventions, including the ones that saw the incredible leap in technology from the invention of the first practical bicycle by Baron Karl von Drais in 1817 straight to the first car by Karl Benz in 1886, both in Germany.

The world wasn't ready for automobiles when they arrived. People walked in front of them, shooing horses and pedestrians out of the way. But just like stairs and elevators, they changed the way we lived.

Cars connected cities and countries, allowing the delivery of food, post and people far quicker than was possible before. Just like penthouse apartments, they became a status symbol for the new capitalists.

They got bigger, bolder and sexier, creating industries that power economies. Until we hit a plateau.

As demand for cars grew, we started making them smaller, more affordable and easier to drive – but the fundamentals of cars didn't really change from the days of Karl Benz until just a few years ago, as the modern tech revolution merged with our awareness of the consequences of widespread use of internal combustion engines.

Apps like Uber, Lyft and Taxify, hybrid electric engines and even flexible working hours are a response to our reliance on cars, designed to reduce our impact – and that's just the beginning. AI is going to change the automotive industry just as the elevator changed cityscapes and property values.

Most of the world's major car manufacturers are developing autonomous vehicles because they know that self-driving cars, planes, buses and trains spell the end for self-driven transport. Think about the knock-on effect: fewer single-passenger cars means less traffic and reduced emissions. The rage-fuelling commute you face today will be replaced with an opportunity to attend virtual meetings, work, sleep and network in comfort while you're being safely ferried to your office – when you're not working from home, that is.

Thanks to virtual reality, remote work will mean that we can do anything from home (or the car).

We will value space more than a car or the proximity to an industry – plus, living further out will offer privacy and peace, and there will, ironically, be value in a productive commute. Suddenly larger suburban properties will become more desirable.

People search 'time' twice as much as they search 'money' on Google, so it's safe to say it's high on our list of priorities. Living in the suburbs does the impossible and makes time for us: time that is beyond precious when the world is moving at breakneck speed.

||||||||||||||||||||||||||||||||||||||||||||||||||||||||||||||||||||||||||||||||| ||||

THE BOTTOM LINE

The phasing of driverless cars into our daily life – a process that has already begun – will have certain quite obvious ramifications. They will ease the stress of commuting and make driving safer. (Insurance premiums will drop.) Over time, they will ease traffic congestion. That will be PLAINsight before too long. FOREsight comes in understanding – now – the greater changes that are coming. Just as the elevator created a demand for premium-priced penthouse apartments decades ago, autonomous vehicles are going to have a direct impact on the price of property away from city centres. What opportunities will this present?

nost notorious corners

ut here is a feature rare

on your left, its many g

om with a slight degree

aving a crisp adow, t

verlapping agged s

the house, the cantil
noticed. the afternoo
sspieces make the on
variation. Underneat
additive parallax dra
puettes

magical
language

HOW THE WORDS YOU USE CAN,
LITERALLY CHANGE YOUR LIFE

Your beliefs become your thoughts.
Your thoughts become your words.
Your words become your actions.
Your actions become your habits.
Your habits become your values.
Your values become your destiny.

Mahatma Gandhi was spot on wtih these words, revealing that what we think and say – our thoughts and words – determine who we become. For me, language is a superpower that can set us up to flourish in the future – if we choose our words wisely. I love Gandhi's quote, but I prefer to think of it like this:

Our language becomes our rituals.
Our rituals become our habits.
Our habits become our behaviours.
Our behaviours become our personality.
Our personality becomes our personal reality.

HINDSIGHT

Language is probably the most powerful force ever used to shape, develop and inspire mankind. It literally allowed us to make history and then to record it (preserving our HINDsight). Since the beginning of time, we've told stories around fires, etched myths into human consciousness and used words to change the world. But persuasive language is not just the plaything of poets and politicians. We use words to woo lovers, teach children and keep ourselves entertained with plays, songs and books.

Once radio and TV gave us the power to broadcast messages to wide audiences, the power of language was amplified: we could make ideas feel electric by combining words in the right way, and disseminate them around the world in a flash. The internet has only amplified that amplification. Whether it's videos or vlogs, Twitter or TikTok, our words are everywhere, and they're more powerful than ever.

PLAINSIGHT

Language offers a mirror on the state of society. Victorians were rigid and formal, and so was their syntax. Fast-forward to the summer of love, and language became a lot more chilled and groovy.

You don't need to learn linguistics to use words to track society, though, because every generation is marked in time and place by its slang – and it's a glimpse into that world. When I was younger, we called bad guys *spodes*, and *gronsch* meant kiss... 'nuff said.

Today's slang is all about speed. Emojis and hashtags are the hi-tech hieroglyphs of a generation that's always moving. We're too busy to talk, so we text. In shorthand. OMG, we're quick. We have FOMO because YOLO. (Try JOMO.) If things are really serious, we might send a voicenote.

It's a sign of the times: we're connected to more people than ever before, and we need to communicate quickly and clearly with all of them 24/7. But I believe a key contributor to this way of communication comes from forgetting that the language we use is, quite literally, magic.

INSIGHT

If you follow me online – thank you, by the way – you may know that I'm a big fan of Dr Joe Dispenza, a neuroscientist and thought leader who explores our influence on the quantum fields around us, and our ability to create our own reality. At a relatively simple level, he encourages a practice he calls 'creating your day', when you start your day by thinking about what you want to achieve. Language then becomes the tool for making that vision real.[1]

> THE KEY UNDERSTANDING IS THAT
> THE LANGUAGE WE USE IS NOT JUST
> AN ARBITRARY DESCRIPTION OF WHAT
> IS HAPPENING TO US AND AROUND US; IT
> DETERMINES THE VERY WORLD WE LIVE IN.

That's worth reading again.

When we're stuck in PLAINsight, we walk around saying what we see without giving it a second thought – even though what we say and how we say it can be as critical in shaping our future as what we think. In fact, it changes the *way* we think.

'Wow, that's so expensive...' 'Air travel is such a nightmare...' 'My workers are so lazy...' 'My boss is an asshole!' 'You know, the government...'

This is how we communicate: without thinking. And most of the time that's fine. But often we miss opportunities, when the language we use has the potential to offer great positive power in our life.

FORESIGHT

For most of us, the way we speak and the words we use are a habit hardwired into who we are. I say 'bru' instead of 'bro' because I spend more time in Cape Town than in LA. I'm sure you make similar unconscious language choices wherever you may be. If we were really motivated to change them – if, for instance, I moved to LA and felt I needed to call people 'bro' instead of 'bru' – we could.

To fully benefit from Dr Dispenza's process, we need to be doing exactly that: changing our habits and unlearning the way we work with words.

Time to go back to school.

When we get to school the first thing we learn is how to spell. But what is a spell? It's an enchantment created to change something. Once we've mastered our ABCs, we're taught how to put words into sentences. And every time we speak, we are *sentencing* ourselves to the magic *spells* we've chosen to use to create the world we live in.[2]

I don't believe these wordplays are a coincidence.

When we use language that is intentional and clear, we build a different world for ourselves. (Different words = different worlds.) We stop complaining about things being expensive, because that word moves things out of our reach. We stop calling our employees lazy, because when we do we reinforce low expectations. We don't complain about traffic or our boss or crooked politicians, because what we say becomes our reality.

I'm not asking you to start speaking like a human dictionary or to sign up with the grammar police; but I do recommend you express your goals and ambitions in a clear, intentional way.

I heard a profound example of this on Cal Fussman's *Big Questions* podcast.[3] He was interviewing the founder of period-proof underwear company THINX, Miki Agrawal, about her new book, the brilliantly titled *Disrupt-her*.[4]

In the book, Agrawal speaks about the word 'fail'. Failure has become a modern rallying call; it's wrapped into brand slogans and mantras like 'fail forward' or 'fail harder', and there is certainly some value in that. But Agrawal argues that the word itself carries negative energy with it, regardless of how it's used. She suggests that we replace 'failure' with 'revelation'. A superb idea. Instead of saying 'My last relationship was a failure', we might say, 'My last relationship was a revelation, and I know what to do next time.' (See SHOT 18 for more on this.)

Following this line of thinking, I am particular about the language that I use to sentence myself to the magic spells I cast. I recommend it.

THE BOTTOM LINE

Choosing your words wisely is a simple path to changing your outlook and attitude, which will ultimately present you with better opportunities and shift your reality. It will allow you to build the foundation of flexibility and fluidity you need to face the future.

Being intentional about what you say starts to build the neural pathways that become habits; habits that overflow into every aspect of your life to prepare you for a profound future where we use words to describe, and create, our abundant world.

[3]

THE GOLD STANDARD OF RECYCLING
WHY GOLD WILL STAY IMPORTANT, BUT GOLD MINES WON'T

HINDSIGHT

Gold. It's inspired myths, given birth to overnight cities, fuelled wars and bankrolled economies. We've been pulling gold out of the ground and turning it into jewellery and currency for 7,000 years[1], but there's far more to it than its inherent shiny value. It's a remarkably useful metal, an inert and malleable conductor that dentists, glass-makers and aerospace engineers have been partial to across the ages.

Gold crowns winners, sanctifies weddings and validates award-winning songs. So much of human history has been influenced by it in some way.

PLAINSIGHT

Gold is so commonplace and familiar that we've started to lose sight of its value.

We all know that it's shiny and nice to look at, but most of us don't really understand why it's useful, what it's used for, or even where it comes from. It's now little more than a price index in the finance section of the evening news (if you happen to watch the news, that is – which I strongly advise against[*]).

---

[*] I made a conscious decision to stop watching the news in 2011. CNN may as well stand for Crisis News Network, in my opinion, and we need far less random anxiety in our lives. Better to go online and get the targeted news that's relevant to your life when you need it.

Half the time gold isn't even *gold* any more. Modern jewellery trends have taken a shining to rose and white gold, even though the name itself comes from the Germanic word *gulþa* meaning the colour gold, and the Old English *geolu* for yellow. Meanwhile, other precious metals such as platinum and palladium have eaten into its share of the jewellery market.

It's fair to say that gold has lost its novelty – and it's because we've taken it for granted that it's an ideal candidate for disruption.

INSIGHT

Today, gold adds key value to prominent industries. It's the electric heart conducting the show in critical medical technology, manufacturing machines and your smartphone. In fact, almost all sophisticated electronic devices contain a small amount of gold.[2]

33% OF ALL GOLD AND SILVER MINED GLOBALLY IS USED IN ELECTRONICS.
1 TON OF CELLPHONES CONTAINS MORE GOLD THAN 70 TONS OF GOLD ORE.
1 BILLION CELLPHONES ARE SOLD A YEAR.
THERE ARE MORE RARE EARTH METALS IN LANDFILLS THAN IN ALL GLOBAL RESERVES.
TODAY, LESS THAN 1% OF RARE EARTH METALS IS RECYCLED.

And here's the kicker:

4,000 TONS OF E-WASTE ARRIVES
AT GIUYI IN CHINA EVERY HOUR – AND
OUR DEVICES ARE BEING REBORN.

These staggering numbers, from a presentation by my fellow Singularity alum David Roberts, will do a lot more than help you spice up your next dinner party.[3] They are living proof of FOREsight in action.

FORESIGHT

A new generation of electronic entrepreneurs has started recycling gold and rare earth metals from discarded devices – and these innovators are quite literally sitting on a new type of gold mine.

E-waste dumps where our old iPhones and laptops go to die are loaded with enough precious materials to completely disrupt the mining sector and, unlike dwindling natural resources, this gold mine is growing.

Harvesting old gold is faster, safer, simpler, cheaper and less harmful to the environment than traditional techniques, and it appears it will be sustainable, given the rate at which we go through electronic devices. It's not unimaginable that we could keep recycling gold in a perpetual loop, eventually weaning us off our need for traditional mining altogether.

This shift to recycling rather than mining isn't limited to tech, either. The upcoming 2020 Olympic Games in Tokyo will showcase medals made entirely from metals from e-waste.[4]

The same recycling approach applies to many metals now, such as aluminium, brass and copper. In a similar vein, diamonds may be forever, but now we don't need to wait that long for them to be compressed and mined, and to make their way onto that important finger next to the pinkie: they can be grown in laboratories or simply squeezed into existence by powerful machinery.

This all points to:

☐ Bad news for the various mining industries.

☐ Good news for the environment.

RECYCLING 2.0

Industries that harm the environment will increasingly fall out of favour, because modern generations are done turning a blind eye. Consumers are demanding transparency about where their food comes from, what happens to plastic, and who exactly is producing their clothes. Cult brands are using this shift to fuel their business. It's conscious capitalism at its best: harm is reduced across the business chain, ideally to nothing, and it's done in a way so that profits don't suffer.

Led by its CEO Yvon Chouinard's passion for the environment, outdoor clothing brand Patagonia donates 10% of its profits or 1% of the company's total sales (whichever is greater) to environmental groups. In 2018 it even gave the $10 million tax break it received from the Trump administration to environmental protection causes.[5]

In 2017, Adidas collaborated with the Parley environmental movement against ocean plastic pollution: the partnership saw the production and sales of one million pairs of shoes made from recycled ocean plastic. As with Patagonia, this isn't about hopping on a trend for a moment in time; the apparel manufacturer has pledged to make all of its shoes from the material by 2030.[6]

More recently, scientists in Japan accidentally created an enzyme that 'eats' the PET plastic used to make soft-drink bottles. This could pave the way for recycling clear plastic bottles back into clear plastic bottles, and end the need to produce new plastic.[7]

Despite the fact that straws account for less than 1% of the plastic waste in our oceans, the #NoStraw movement has caught on to the point where sundowners made to be sipped through straws are falling out of favour[8] – as a result, Champagne is making a bubbly comeback. Sales hit record highs in 2018 according to trade body Comité Champagne.[9] More serious challenges that need addressing are, for example, the discarded fishing equipment that accounts for nearly half of the North Atlantic garbage patch[10] and the 10 rivers that contribute more than a quarter of our oceans' annual plastic pollution*, both of which kill millions of animals and fish every year – but straws are a good start, and are a sign of movements to come.

IIIIIIIIIIIIIIIIIIIIIIIIIIIIIIIIIIIIIIIIIIIIIIIIIIIIIIIIIIIIIIIIIIII IIII

THE BOTTOM LINE

Even though these examples come from different sectors, they all reflect a shift in consumer thinking. PLAINsight and ignorant bliss are dead. Being eco-conscious has shifted from being a fringe fascination to the building block of modern business. Bamboo toothbrushes and biodegradable beer rings are only the start of our sustainable future, and using the 'reuse, recycle' movement to future-proof your finances and make sure you're doing good business makes good business sense. The way we 'mine' gold is just the tip of the iceberg.

---

*The 10 rivers are, in descending order, the Yangtze, Indus, Yellow, Hai, Nile, Ganges, Pearl, Amur, Niger and Mekong. Together, they contribute more than 90% of global river-borne plastic pollution.[11]

FOCUS ON FLEX APPEAL

THE EDUCATION WE NEED
FOR FUTURE SUCCESS

[4]

HINDSIGHT

If I had a dollar for every time someone's asked me what aspect of their life they should focus on to make sure they're fighting-fit for the future... Next time I'm asked, I'll point to this page.

In my experience, the single most inhibiting factor that prevents us becoming future-ready is our acceptance of the familiar – 'the plan'. We inherit the plan from our parents, and their parents and *their* parents before them, and on and on.

In their time, 'success' was standardised. You had to go to school, get into university, where ideally you coupled up, get a degree to get you a job, then start the slow climb up the corporate ladder until you got a (mined) gold watch on retirement. Yawn...

From the dawn of the Industrial Revolution until not too long ago that was par for the course, and it became the basis of unprecedented global economic growth, slowly and steadily transforming human existence. But it's hardly exciting. In fact, it's not far removed from that sleepy Mediterranean village we discussed in the opening pages: a formula for getting by on safety and security instead of unlocking the boundless possibilities of an exponential world.

This grind generated progress over the centuries, but at a scale and speed that cannot match the pace of today. We had entire generations going through the motions before; now we need inspired leaps.

PLAINSIGHT

Most parents, particularly those in more traditional countries and communities, still teach their children to follow a set plan: study hard, earn one of the 'approved' degrees, find a suitable partner. There's a little more leeway these days, but the basics are the same. And the intentions are good: they want their kids to have a chance at a better life, and they see this as the best way forward.

Problem is, the plan hasn't changed with the times. What worked for past generations is no longer guaranteed to work today. 'The plan' is now a likely route to stagnation, and the world is moving away from it, especially with the growing disillusionment about modern universities.

In recent years, the insidious problem of student debt has made regular headlines, while the disturbing new age of campus politics has become a prominent topic of debate. Most profoundly, though, the relevance and effectiveness of a university education has come under the spotlight. Following the publication of a 2014 Gallup and Purdue University study of 30,000 American graduates, CEO of the College Board in the US David Coleman sums up the nub of the problem: 'Only 3% of students [in the 2010s] have the kind of transformative experience in college that fosters personal success and happiness.' This number was 26% in the 1960s, and has been decreasing steadily.[1]

Famous varsity dropouts like Bill Gates, Steve Jobs and Mark Zuckerberg are proof that you can succeed if you apply yourself to what really excites you and take the opportunity when it presents itself. My favourite personal example comes in the form of my friend Mark Sham, who teaches large multinational organisations about the future of education even though he never finished high school.

As a result of all this, parents are starting to accept that a degree is not a necessity for life success. In certain professions – the STEM fields, for instance – a degree understandably still holds sway; but in others, particularly business, it may well hold you back.

Let me emphasise: I'm not deriding the notions of education or bettering ourselves; exactly *how* we do it is the question. The danger we face today is in falling into a cycle where we worry about degrees and certificates instead of learning how to recognise our authentic selves and identify opportunities.

INSIGHT

In the past, education really was a privilege; now it's a universal right. In functioning societies everyone is educated to a point, and the common strategy to stand out from the crowd and compete within the global job market is for more: more degrees, more courses, more qualifications. Right now, there are beauty therapists, personal trainers, accountants and financial managers piling on the professional papers to make their CVs sparkle – because that's what's expected.

But do all of those extra qualifications help?

They may help you get to grips with a particular skill, but the people who are really succeeding aren't spending every spare second in weekend classes or poring over outdated ideas. They have activated all their INsight and academic knowledge to understand what genius lies inside them and what invisible dots they can connect. This is not a process of relying on what you've been told might be useful and collecting a lottery of possible careers; it's about understanding what excites you and forging a process that leads into the future.

FORESIGHT

I repeat: it's admirable to be the best you can be, but chasing the affirmation of others by stockpiling degrees has distracted us from focusing on our consciousness. Please remember:

ACCOMPLISHMENT DOES NOT EQUAL PURPOSE. BUT PURPOSE LEADS YOU INTO THE FUTURE.

Before you commit to your next online course, you need to start defining your purpose. I recommend you start by answering these questions:

What is your relationship with your past like?
What is your relationship with responsibility like?
What is your relationship with money like?
What is your relationship with influence, power and force like?

What is your relationship with your past like?
How do you handle your pesky past? If you've read either of my previous books, you'll know how much emphasis I place on the importance of healing your past, a familiar refrain that reappears in these pages.

If you haven't healed from the pain and escaped HINDsight, you'll approach the working world from a place of low energy. When that happens, you're going to fall into a pattern of unhappiness, no matter how well qualified you are. You'll find you attract abusive bosses, work for less than you're worth, and continuously question yourself. That happens because you're repeating the patterns you remember, and end up seeking the familiar without even realising it.

What is your relationship with responsibility like?

All the qualifications in the world won't shield us from stepping up when we need to, in particular in times of hardship. We need to be confident enough in our ability, not our background, to make sure we can handle whatever comes our way.

What is your relationship with money like?

Money itself isn't the root of all evil; it can be a powerful tool for tomorrow.

The full quote is, of course, 'The *love of* money is the root of all evil.' It becomes an issue when we follow negative patterns purely for a big paycheque. And remember, a massive salary won't automatically immunise you from the way technology is going to evolve your job and industry.

The other side of the coin is the avoidance of effective and responsible money management, a guaranteed drain on energy and consciousness. If you're always coming up short at month-end and putting off paying bills, it's time to confront your financial situation with honesty.

What is your relationship with influence, power and force like?

The late Dr David Hawkins, a writer, physician and psychiatrist who explored consciousness, had a profound impact on defining the difference between power and force. In his lecture 'Transcending the mind', Hawkins argued that force is immature: a toddler lashing out mid-tantrum.[2] When we force anything, we generate counterforce and resistance (that's Newton's Laws 101). It delivers quick, instant, short-term changes, but that energy quickly dissipates – like our influence when we try to force people into certain action.

Power, on the other hand, is aligned to truth and integrity. Gravity is a good example: it is ever-present and has no opposition. When we act with power, we influence the world, but not in the immediate, causal way we're used to: the results of our action take more time, but last far longer. The use of power is a sign of a mature, confident person with a clear vision.

To be influential, we need to inspire others, using power instead of force. Do you try to force your way forward, or have you developed your consciousness to the point where you trust your own power?

Pencils down. How did you do?

These questions are the entrance exam to finding out how flexible your perspective is. Work on your relationships with your past, with responsibility, with money and with influence, power and force. The most valuable course you can do in a changing world is to study yourself. So study what makes you tick and focus on what makes you excited; that's going to qualify you to face the future.

THE BOTTOM LINE

'The plan' was safe, but it comes from a past when fitting in and following due process was the ideal – a perspective that is far from foolproof today. The keys now, in our entrepreneurial, fast-evolving age, are an understanding of exactly who you are and where you're going, and a flexibility of mind to keep you on track. Paper qualifications are secondary to the emotional qualifications that provide you with flexibility, fluidity and a fresh perspective.

Ready to take off the training wheels? The rest of the SHOTs in the book are a little more flexible and fluid than the starting four – which, as we've just seen, is important. Keep an eye out for key words that relate to each type of sight, and let them guide you as you develop your ability to see invisible patterns.

[5]

DISRUPTING
YOURSELF

WHY TODAY, TOMORROW AND
FUTURE TEAMS ARE CRITICAL
TO LONG-TERM SUCCESS

Everyone in corporate has sat in a war-room session at some point. You know the deal: the big boss, almost definitely a guy, sits everyone down and paints a bleak picture of sales and quarterly profit declines. Then he slams his fist on the table and opens the floor for business-saving ideas.

Cue the crickets.

I suffered through one of these sessions recently. A South African business made up of thousands of franchisees was asking its people to innovate from within, and it wasn't going well.

In business, ideas can come from anywhere, so asking for advice from people who work on the ground may seem like a good idea. But in this case, the franchisees hadn't invested in the brand because they wanted to introduce fresh thinking to the mix; they had invested in the stability and familiarity of an existing model. Looking to them for inspiration and innovation was a sign of desperation.

Unsurprisingly, frustration levels at the workshop ran particularly high. The franchisees were feeling the pressure, and the franchisors weren't getting the gritty flashes of genius they'd hoped for.

Want to avoid those awkward boardroom silences? Then you need to bring consumers, trend experts and transformation specialists into your business – *before* the warning bells start ringing – to fly the flag for flexibility.

READY, SET, HACK

Five years from now, Millennials won't be a misunderstood demographic with a new perspective: they will be the world's strongest spending force, and a critical part of the team you need to build for tomorrow. It's time businesses started respecting their opinions.

Consumers can tell you what they like and don't like; they're a living, breathing barometer to test trends for relevance. Showing them what's happening within and outside your sector, and what new products you're planning, will help you gauge what's likely to work.

It's also valuable to bring Millennial employees into the fold: they can represent the needs of the younger market, and serve as a useful filter when planning the future direction of your business. Creating a Millennial board – as Deloitte has done – can reveal new realities about your market.

But when it comes to building a business designed to adapt, you can't beat a hackathon.

A what-a-thon?

A hackathon is a competition where creatives, futurists and technologists develop possible solutions to specific business problems. This isn't about efficiency. The light bulb wasn't invented by making the candle more efficient; it required brand-new thinking. A hackathon is about innovation and disruption to create progress once efficiency has hit its ceiling. The organisation funds the best solution to see where it leads, and the team that developed it can either stick around through its implementation, or move on to the next project.

Once you know which idea you're going to follow, you need a crack team of creative thinkers, operating alongside your primary business, to put it into action. Congrats, you have a sideline start-up! When it starts building momentum, add a key person from your existing business to the team, and keep growing it.

The exceptional business strategist John Hagel calls this process 'scaling the edges'.[1] The trick is to build the business on the edges, funding these initiatives totally until they're big enough to come back and help you disrupt your own industry.

STRUCTURED TO SUCCEED

To make your hack work, you're going to need three teams.

Today's team – the Innovation Team

The first team is tasked with solving the problems you face today; its horizon is the next year or two. It monitors trends to keep things innovative – and yes, a lot of what it does involves making the current working processes that much more efficient.

Tomorrow's team – the Disruption Team

The second team is focused on the kind of changes you will need to adopt to benefit from the major disruptions that we're likely to see in the next two to five years. It is led by data scientists and specialists in AI, blockchain and other cutting-edge technologies relevant to your industry; people who can build business models that could make your current ones obsolete. Efficiency is now a minor consideration.

The day-after team – the Revolution Team

Lastly, you need a small group with free rein to find the future of your business by confronting and contextualising trends, and working towards a future five to 10 years from now (which will be completely different to anything we know). Efficiency no longer applies.

This may sound extreme, but new structures are essential to tackling the tomorrow we're busy building right now. The alternative is to keep our perspective on processes that improve speed and efficiency only – if you're not convinced, a little time travel will prove just how dangerous that can be.

BUSINESSES BLIND TO TOMORROW

Legend has it that, in the 1880s, there was a company that produced ox wagon wheels so well that it was struggling to meet demand. But two new technologies were making the company a little nervous: the combustion engine and the expanding railroads. Might they threaten the business?

The company called in an innovation specialist for help. He advised moving towards a more futuristic product, but the board decided it was too much effort to overhaul its production processes and transform the business. The consultant was dismissed.

After a short bout of depression, he founded a company to make rubberised, pneumatic tyres. His name was John Boyd Dunlop, the Scot credited with 'realising rubber could withstand the wear and tear of being a tyre while retaining its resilience', and changing our world in the process.[2]

More recently, razor giant Gillette almost suffered the same fate as the ox wagon companies of the 19th century. In the first decade of the new millennium, the company found itself trapped in an innovation loop, adding more pointless blades whenever it felt it needed to demonstrate its relevance to the market. The higher the number, the larger the gap it was opening beneath its feet – and so the Dollar Shave Club burst onto the scene. Founded in California in 2011, the start-up offered a monthly subscription service selling single-blade razors for as little as a dollar a month. After just five years of business, it sold to Unilever for $1 billion.[3]

A similar thing happened to Nokia. Just over 10 years ago, it had a billion customers around the world. When it re-released the iconic 3310 in 2017, no-one cared. In six years, Nokia plummeted from industry-leading $100-billion giant to forgotten $7-billion business[4] – a decline that saw the board in tears, simply because it had prioritised efficiency and incremental innovation over real disruption.

In the disruptive world of today, these cases are a dime a dozen. They prove that even the best businesses will fail if they innovate for innovation's sake, or get so caught up in efficiency that they lose their direction.

||||||||||||||||||||||||||||||||||||||||||||||||||||||||||||||||||||||| ||||

THE BOTTOM LINE

To survive and thrive today, businesses need a systematic approach to future assessment, covering the short, medium and long term. The respective teams need to focus in their time frames only, with different emphasis on efficiency versus innovation and disruption, the ultimate keys to success.

This is a move that forces you to build a new, different business, and learn different skills as needed – the definition of adaptability and future-fitness that sets you up to pursue the potential that our 'impossible' tomorrow presents.

6

FINDING
FORGIVENESS

Facing your past in order to develop
empathy with others

[6]

There are mantras and moments that affect our perception of the world around us and strike home like a thunderclap. It might be a quote on Facebook, a brand slogan or something a friend says; it just seems to stick with you. For me, an idea as subtle and simple as it is easy to remember set me on my path:

> WE ARE THE ARCHITECTS OF THE REALITY THAT WE ARE CONSTANTLY CREATING, AND WE NEED TO BECOME CONSCIOUS OF THIS POWER.

I doubt that most people apply this thinking in their lives, and to that point in mine I certainly hadn't. Generally, we believe we are at the mercy of circumstance, and we play the hand we're dealt.

But finding purpose when you think your future's been written for you is almost impossible, because it makes you feel like you have no free will. And because *que sera sera*, it's easy to accept that you can only do so much – or as little as you want – to build the life you want to live.

Since I first thought hard about the possibility of creating the reality I wanted, I've spent as much time as possible researching, learning about and talking about what it takes to get to a place where I can wield that power responsibly. I always take note when I come across instances of it in action.

For instance, I had the privilege of listening to a conversation not long ago, in which an American man was talking to a spiritual guru from India. The man said that, upon meeting the guru, he felt as if the guru could see his whole past and entire future – and still love him, still accept him 100% for who he was. The power of this wholehearted acceptance stuck with me. It seemed that the guru wasn't affected by the negative elements of other people – their difficult moods, volatile temperaments or the mistakes they'd made – because he had confronted and overcome his own past in its entirety.

The lesson seemed clear: once we have faced our past and forgiven ourselves for it, we are able to show empathy towards other people and their past, and accept them for who they are in the present moment. This means we aren't as easily triggered by their perceived shortcomings or, more accurately, by the expectations we project onto them.

Think of it like this: if you have a crack in your spectacles, every morning when you look at yourself in the mirror you will face a distorted version of yourself. And when you look out at the world, it too will be distorted. You'll never see the real you or the real world until those spectacles are fixed. It's the same with your past:

UNTIL YOU CAN HEAL THE WOUNDS
THAT HOLD YOU BACK, YOU WON'T
SEE YOURSELF, OR THE PEOPLE
IN YOUR LIFE, AS WHOLE.

As I've grown my brand over the years, I've had the pleasure of watching my team grow with it. By projecting the best version of myself onto my team, I have tried to help them see what they can become to their absolute capacity. And I have encouraged them to do the reverse to me.

But you can only project what you truly believe about yourself.

I've learnt to see the bigger potential within myself. I'm sure not claiming to be a spiritual guru, but I do try to accept where the people I work with come from – and I can only do this by trying to accept myself more and more every day. (A never-ending process.)

'With forgiveness, your victim identity dissolves, your true power emerges... Instead of blaming the darkness you bring in the light.'
ECKHART TOLLE, author and spiritual teacher

FORGIVENESS IS THE KEY

Call it inspiration, enthusiasm or 'espirito', being excited about the future comes down to forgiveness of the past. Once we forgive ourselves, we can project that forgiveness onto others, and start creating the future we really want, rather than one created by our unhealed projections.

A man who has had an enormous impact on my understanding of the power of forgiveness is Dr Joe Dispenza, who we've already met in these pages. I devour his work, and strongly recommend his live workshops. Every time I interact with his thinking, I learn something new.

One notion he keeps describing is the danger of living a repetitive life based on our history and memories. This correlates well with my concept of HINDsight: the danger of being reliant on memories is that they lead us to repeat the same patterns and make the same mistakes. They can distort our PLAINsight with a negative lens, and taint our INsight to a point where we are too set in our ways to activate knowledge and generate FOREsight.

Only once we confront our memories can we start making plans for our future, both in our personal life and in business.

A personal example I have shared before is worth repeating here.

My relationship with my dad has always been tricky. To this day, I don't know if he'll ever deal with his shadows, or become the person a son expects his father figure to be – an impossible ideal, I imagine. What I do know is that if I don't accept him for who he is right now, our relationship in the future will be nothing more than a continuation of my past.

I've realised that I need to forgive him and forget the idea that he isn't perfect. (No-one is!) That realisation has set me free to follow my highest passion. By addressing my own perspective, I've created a platform for the two of us to forge a better future, together.

Where to start

Dealing with your past is easier said than done, and generally an ongoing process – but the gift of perspective it brings is profound. Spend the time identifying what's hurt you, and which memories seem to be stuck on repeat: do this with a coach or a therapist, use meditation, write in a journal, share with your partner, or simply use any process that works for you. I found great insight and ultimately forgiveness in 'teacher plants', like Ayahuasca and San Pedro, which opened my heart and mind and allowed me to face the past shadows I'd tried so hard to bury.

Whatever works for you, do it.

I feel so strongly about the process of understanding the memories that haunt us that I frequently write about it and discuss it in my talks. You'll see references throughout this book – not least the idea of moving away from HINDsight – and I recommend reading the chapter on Micro Inspection in my previous book *Magnetiize* if you're interested in exploring this in more detail.

||||||||||||||||||||||||||||||||||||||||||||||||||||||||||||||||| ||||

THE BOTTOM LINE

The question at the heart of this SHOT is simple, but unbelievably important: are you living a life based on a set of repeated memories, trapped in HINDsight – or are you defining yourself by connecting the invisible dots towards the future you want?

To create your reality and become the person you want to be, you need to make deliberate, intentional choices every moment of every day. The first one is to forgive your past, stop looking back and start looking forward. Once you do, you'll find yourself able to make choices that connect the dots between the present and your greatest potential. You'll be able to make the leap from HINDsight to FOREsight.

NGING
THE
GAME

HOW TO LEAD WHEN DISRUPTION
REWRITES THE RULES

[7]

In his book *Outliers*, the wild-haired Malcolm Gladwell wrote that it takes 10,000 hours to master a skill.[1] It wasn't his theory, but he made it popular.

Somehow, it's a number that's slipped into the collective consciousness, and the concept behind it seems to hold water. It's obvious to most people that it takes commitment, hard work and dedication to become great. In fact, I'm pretty sure that all the famous greats, from Rembrandt to Ronaldo, have spent more than the 416 days of constant practice, as defined by Gladwell, in their pursuit of the pinnacle.

While some may quibble over the number itself, the concept highlights a deeper question in today's disruptable world. Is the idea of mastering one skill and building your whole business or career on its back still a worthy idea?

SPORTING CHANCES VS REAL LIFE

Think of some of the greats of sport: Martina Navratilova, Michael Jordan, Lionel Messi and similar superhumans. Barring none, they all spent countless hours rising to the top of their game – hitting balls, throwing balls, kicking balls; studying the greats, finding weakness in their opponents; exploring everything about technology, technique and nutrition – to get the fractional advantage they needed to become the best. In combination with their natural talent, it was that incredible effort that put them among the greatest players of all time.

Success in the realm of professional sport is, however, increasingly divergent from real-world success: an artificial arena with absolute regulation of rules, where the utmost dedication to one approach is the ultimate differentiator. But imagine if the rules were overhauled one day, allowing players to use electronic exoskeletons and jetpacks. That's what's happening to the business world as we know it.

The problem with holding on to the 10,000-hour rule is that we think logging that amount of time immunises our lives and businesses against change. As we see repeated in other SHOTs, this is because we've been following the deep footprints of our grandparents. In their time, people spent their entire life mastering one skill, because it automatically put them ahead of the competition. We've now been led to believe that because we've paid our dues, we're in the same position; that making a lifelong commitment to one field is enough to secure a career.

Repeating the patterns we've inherited is a natural result of the linear thinking that's hardwired into the human condition. We go from A to B, and from B to C, progressing from point to point until we die.

Build a shelter. Start a fire. Find food. It's difficult to decode thousands of years of programming, so we resist it: we use HINDsight to defend our position and stick to the 'that's the way we've always done it' story, even when it inhibits the freedom of choice we have earned as a species to live the exact life we want.

Apart from limiting our awesome potential, this perspective is becoming increasingly risky. With the current rate of change, we might one day wake up in a completely different world.

In the course of writing my book, a musical algorithm called Endel has been signed to Warner Music[2], the same record label that represents the world's favourite ginger superstar singer/songwriter Ed Sheeran.

The algorithm uses the circadian rhythms that regulate your body's sleep cycles, the musical structures of the pentatonic scale, and data such as your heart rate and the weather at your geographical location to create sounds that help you focus, or sleep, or chill.

That's just a drop in the ocean of disruption. An AI newsreader in China is so 'human', it's almost impossible to tell he isn't a real person.[3] Another AI, known as Sophia, has been granted honorary citizenship in Saudi Arabia.[4] It's impossible to keep track of all the innovation in the world, which means we can never assume that technology isn't going to turn our world upside down overnight.

In the same way, we can't assume that making a 10,000-hour commitment to learning a fixed skill will prevent new developments from having a massive impact on the way we learn, live and love one another. Or that progress, in whatever field we specialise in, will happen in a straight line.

NON-LINEAR, AUDACIOUS ACTION

Our world and the rules that govern it are changing at an exponential rate, so we need to focus our energy on learning to be flexible and adaptable enough to keep up. (See SHOTs 4 and 10.) We need to start thinking in exponential ways.

Living an exponential life is about being audacious enough to leave linear thinking behind, and start with the end in mind. Once you have set the right goals and know exactly what you want your life to mean, you can work backwards to plot a path that will get you there. Because you can clearly see Z, you can rearrange the alphabet of your life into a story that ends with you achieving that audacious goal.

Linear thinking has defined the way we do business, too. It's responsible for our insatiable appetite for processes, check lists and organisation.

We can't help it: we love to see things happen step by step.

Breaking news: even if you're using an agile approach or a waterfall structure to cascade information to your team, you're still moving from point A to point B. These are more efficient models, not disruptive models.

When you take an audacious, exponential approach, you start to see businesses at the limit of what's possible today, and build the plans to make yours one of them by connecting invisible dots.

IF THEY CAN DO IT...

Moving from a linear business to an exponential one is not only essential; it's easier and more common than you'd think. One of the world's biggest brands has just done it again.

Apple is already renowned as one of the great disruptors of modern time, entirely transforming the PC, cellphone, music and watch industries (to name the obvious ones). In 2018, it pre-emptively disrupted itself, transforming its entire business model from hardware provider to service platform, and shifting its focus from creating sexy devices with intuitive interfaces to delivering on-demand entertainment.[5] Not a single new device was unveiled at the Apple event in March 2019 when the switch became apparent – but they did launch a credit card and a content-streaming service.

What really stands out about this giant leap for Apple-kind is that the company's current CEO Tim Cook has a background in developing hardware supply chains. His career history is all about figuring out the processes to get hardware from A to B across Asia and eventually the globe. But he saw that future consumers wouldn't need a smartphone with 25 cameras – they'd prefer fresh content and interest-free credit.

It's happening in every industry all around the world, and it's changing the way we define and understand our competitors. In South Africa, the country's premium medical-aid provider, Discovery, has opened a bank, with the aim of linking financial wealth and insurance to your physical health.[6] That's pretty audacious.

Strategist Alberto Brea breaks it down well on his blog:[7]

If you are NBC, your competition is not just Fox, HBO or Netflix. You are competing against Apple, who is launching its own subscription video, gaming, and credit card services. The more people use Apple, the less need to watch NBC.

If you are Visa, your competition is not just Mastercard or AmEx. You are competing against Apple Wallet, Amazon Pay... The more people use digital wallets, the less need for a credit card.

If you are Toyota, your competition is not just Nissan, Honda, GM. You are competing against Uber, Google self-driving cars, Citibikes... The more people use alternative transportation methods, the less need to buy a car.

If you are Canon cameras, your competition is not just Nikon and Sony. You are competing against iPhones, Android phones, tablets... The more people use their phones as cameras, the less need to buy one.

If you are Facebook, your competition is not just Google or Snapchat. You are competing against all the ad-free subscription services (Netflix, Apple, Amazon Prime Video). The more people spend time watching Netflix, the less time they have to watch advertising.

Today's competition can come from anywhere. Anyone can be your competitor. The lines have blurred among media, manufacturers, retailers... The only thing you can do is focus on customer needs.

|||||||||||||||||||||||||||||||||||||||||||||||||||||||||||||||||||||||| ||||

THE BOTTOM LINE

If the people in charge of the world's biggest brands are thinking like this, so must we. We can't let fear hold us back. We can't think in straight lines when the future is fluid and exponential – this is the point of connecting invisible dots. We need to work out where we want to go, and then find our way there.

This is not to say that you shouldn't focus on a particular field of expertise. Specialists are still critical to the exponential future. (See SHOT 11.) But planning, procedures and processes are only useful in that they allow us and our businesses to pursue a purpose. We can't allow our perceived specialisation to restrain us.

Imagine how much you could achieve if you dedicated 10,000 hours to practising agility and curiosity. Granted, you'll (probably) never win a Grand Slam, but you *can* achieve tomorrow what's perceived to be impossible today.

[*8*]
REDEFINING
GREATNESS
HOW TO PREPARE YOURSELF
TO REALISE YOUR GOALS

The **singularity** has been described as a point in the future when technological growth becomes so profound that it affects humanity in ways we can't even conceive now.

One of my proudest achievements to date is that I was the first African faculty member of Singularity University, a think tank committed to preparing the world for the singularity – when machines become smarter than human beings. One year I was in the audience, listening to best-selling authors and genome scientists discussing the future; the next, I was getting ready to step onto the stage and share my own thoughts.

Before everyone arrived that day, I spent some time reflecting on greatness.

As a younger man (I'm still a young man!), I thought greatness was all about money, power and influence – the superficial stuff you see in movies and music videos. It was part of my Teenage Boy Syndrome phase, which, as it does with many people, lasted until I was in my late 20s. (This phase is reasonably self-explanatory, but will make more sense if you've read *Magnetiize*.[1])

Before I could successfully pursue a sustainable career in trend analysis and business strategy, and eventually achieve my goal of joining the Singularity faculty, I had to develop a more mature understanding of greatness. In short, it has nothing to do with broadcasting what you're doing on Instagram or flashing an expensive watch in a club. People on that track are wrapped up in ego and insecurity, seeking recognition before they put in the work. It's the hallmark of an immature, masculine perspective, and it can affect anyone, irrespective of gender.

When I lost the material things I thought defined me as a person, in my late 20s, I was forced to reconsider who I was and what I wanted to achieve in my life. Who was I without the fancy cars and the bulging bank balance?[2]

It has taken me a decade to understand what greatness actually is.

SO, WHAT'S GREATNESS?

In the course of human history, roughly 108 billion beings have breathed the air on our planet. About 7% of them are still alive and kicking[3], including you and me. The other 93% haven't been forgotten, though. The course of human history advances on the progress they made, and we build our perspectives on top of how they saw the world and what they did (even when we shouldn't). Their ideas, efforts and struggles have nudged us, bit by bit, to where we are right now.

For a recent transformative example, consider personal computers. Since PCs were invented in the mid-1970s, countless people have made countless choices and decisions about their development that ultimately made them accessible to the masses and exponentially affected the world in countless ways. Today, PCs are mobile and connected by the internet, and have contributed to vast improvements in global health, wealth and education. As children now learn how to code in classrooms all over the world, we can appreciate the collective effort – and greatness – of this human endeavour.

At any given time, we are all making choices and decisions that will directly affect what is possible for future generations. Greatness is understanding that impact, and becoming the best version of yourself so you can add value to humanity forever.

When we view our life through this lens, it's clear that we can't do it alone, and the myth of the self-made man falls away.

TO TAP INTO OUR OWN GENIUS AND CREATE GREATNESS, WE NEED TO FEED OFF THE COLLECTIVE WISDOM OF THOSE WHO CAME BEFORE US, UNLOCK THE POCKETS OF GENIUS AROUND US, AND ADD A SIGNIFICANT MASS OF INCREMENTAL KNOWLEDGE TO THE COLLECTIVE.

The danger of ambition

To fully embrace this perspective it is important to differentiate between greatness and 'ambition' as it is widely understood – another consequence of operating in HINDsight.

Consider the generations who grew up with the same belief and value systems as everyone else in their neighbourhood or community. They went to the same schools, earned the same qualifications and fought for the same jobs. The only way to stand out in that crowd of similarity was to do whatever it took to climb the ladder faster than everyone else. That was ambition, the sought-after predictor of 'success' in the immature business world from which we are emerging.

Ambition in this sense – as a selfish driver for an individual to rise to the top of an existing system – is famously blind because it can prevent us from seeing the patterns and opportunities that ultimately lead to significance. As these patterns and opportunities become more readily available in the exponential world, old-school ambition for ambition's sake becomes an inhibitor rather than a catalyst.

So our concept of ambition needs to change. When our ambitions are fuelled by love, we become more fluid and collaborative. We recognise that we can have the biggest impact by acting as part of a collective. That kind of ambition, built on a foundation of good, is crucial to forging the future, because it is a source of energy that makes it easy to adapt without losing focus.

GOING BEYOND GOALS

Ever feel like you've failed by not realising your ambitions or achieving your goals within the timeframe you had assigned yourself? Do none of the plans you have for yourself ever seem to work out?

Once you understand what greatness is, you can start to set goals in a new way – a way that doesn't chase after money, titles or perceived power, but rather seeks significance. Rather than using a vague plan that's fuelled by an ambition rooted in HINDsight, this journey starts with a clear purpose, and it connects the invisible dots towards a future built on FOREsight.

Goals that are geared towards greatness excite our mind, body and heart. They feel completely different, and they activate four key changes in our rituals and behaviours:

☐ You automatically follow what shines brightest. The things you watch videos about, read about or want to know more about are little signs from your subconscious about your true interests. Let your heart show you what those are.

☐ You follow your curiosity and dive deeper. Once you've reflected on what you're energised and excited by, learn everything you can about it. Immerse yourself in it, and try to understand the topic or goal through the lenses of HINDsight, PLAINsight and INsight. This will help you activate your FOREsight.

☐ You let interest become excitement. And once you let that excitement take hold of your entire being, you will start to actively turn what you've learnt and seen into something you *live*.

☐ You embrace the flow state and the endless energy it brings, allowing yourself to be swept away by your obsession. Harness that excitement and let it guide you when you set your goals.

‖‖‖ ‖‖‖‖

THE BOTTOM LINE

When you view goals as a path to greatness, you'll also avoid following the paths that don't run from the very heart of who you are. Instead of wanting to tick off 50 things on a bucket list of being, which is likely to set you up for disappointment and self-punishment, you will know which handful of goals to focus on, and in so doing find yourself closer to unlocking the greatness inside you.

[9]

ELEGANT
BUSINESS

FOUR STEPS TO PRE-EMPTING
YOUR CUSTOMERS' NEEDS

'Elegant' is not a word we'd use in the past to describe the ruthless, binary, black-and-white world of business, but I believe it must become our guiding light today – not as in the elegance of a swan, but the elegance of what the Oxford English Dictionary calls 'a pleasingly ingenious and simple solution to a scientific theory of problem'.

Arianna Huffington, founder of *The Huffington Post*, speaks of the concept of 'elegant success', which is, she believes, what happens when you find the balance between order and chaos.

'You don't want too much bureaucracy, hierarchy or rules (i.e. absolute order), but you also don't want to have complete chaos,' she says. When these forces operate in harmony, she believes, you maximise creativity and efficiency.[1]

In our increasingly complex world, elegant solutions will become priceless, and to find them we need to see everything linked to our business through a different lens – starting with the consumer.

PEOPLE POWER

As a business owner back in the day, you didn't have to worry about what your shoppers thought, because they were completely reliant on you. Being successful was as simple as creating an efficient business model that consistently delivered something people needed, and making sure they knew about it. Accurate repetition was enough to ensure success.

This is no longer the case.

Technology has turned this linear process on its head. Whereas our past world saw radio and TV inundating people with advertising, the marketing game is not so logical online, specifically with the deep penetration of social media into our lives.

Now, consumers face ads on pretty much every screen they encounter, and they're fatigued by it all. Traditional advertisers are not as trusted as they once were; word-of-mouth recommendations are far more preferable. In addition, your competitors have access to new technology that makes disruption easier and more likely. They can quietly and quickly open an online store or build an app that directly targets your customers, a move you would have seen coming from a mile off in days gone by. Suddenly your consumers have a variety of options.

The combination of critical customers and cutthroat competition has forced businesses to start fighting for their share of their customers' cash, attention and loyalty. And the best way to do that is to put people first.

Caring for consumers

Care and compassion are, however, not intentions you can easily commodify or code. 'Personalised' emails and annoying chatbots tend not to cut it for the discerning, digitally savvy modern consumer.

The elegant solution is to invest in real people and human interaction, but most businesses don't. They *say* they prioritise people, but they are ultimately guided by their quarterly profits, which tend not to care for them. In succumbing to this outdated way of thinking, they are guilty of unsustainable short-termism; they ignore long-term, cathedral thinking in favour of quick wins and 'low-hanging fruit'.

How far are we willing to go to give the consumers what they want? Is a human being actually reading the feedback emails and Facebook complaints? Are we ready to involve our consumers directly in our strategy, and let them create the next evolution of our business? Ultimately, are we aiming, as Steve Jobs was so good at doing, to give them what they want before they even know they want it?

It's not just your consumers you need to prioritise...

In general, employees are the last people a business worries about. I'm not talking about the technicalities of HR; I'm talking about ensuring they're fulfilled and inspired to give their best. People are increasingly choosing to work at companies that share their values, which means your business needs to stand for something, and give your people something to fight for. In looking after your employees, you stand to boost their productivity *and* make brand ambassadors of them all.

> PUTTING PEOPLE AT THE CENTRE
> OF YOUR BUSINESS IS THE BEST WAY
> TO REINVENT WHAT YOU DO.

Lego vs Toys R Us

You'd think toys are easy to sell, but failed toy giant Toys R Us is proof that you need to think about consumers constantly to avoid falling into the 'same-old' trap.

The company was founded in 1948 by American entrepreneur Charles Lazarus, and initially sold children's furniture. Nine years later, Lazarus shifted his attention to focus exclusively on toys, and Toys R Us soon became a global retail leader. It remained the world's biggest toy seller until 1998, at which point two things happened: Lazarus left as chairman of the company, and Walmart surpassed it as the biggest toy retailer in the US.

It took two decades for the company to decline into bankruptcy. It last saw profit in 2013, and in the quarter closing in April 2017 alone, it lost $164 million, almost $40 million more than in the same period the previous year. It was liquidated in 2018.[2]

Toys R Us did what it could to turn the business around, structuring a long-term debt deal worth $5 billion, closing all locations across North America and Europe, and selling off what it could to third parties. Problem was, Toys R Us hadn't offered consumers a chance to *experience* toys, a critical error in today's retail space (see SHOT 13). Today it is a shattered figment of its former glory.

In South Africa, Edcon is a company that I see walking a similar path. Once an industry leader, its Edgars, Jet and CNA stores are considered mall anchor tenants but have been in the doldrums for years, needing regular business rescue while management 'restructures its finance' and generally rearranges the deck chairs. No-one seems to realise that the experience of shopping in an Edgars, Jet or CNA store is almost depressing – that's where they should be starting their revival.

Compare this to Lego, a company that was on the slide in the early 2000s. Lego didn't look back on Christmas sales data and pray for a seasonal spike. Instead, the brand overhauled itself. It replaced its CEO and started to think about what people wanted from its products, cutting the lines that weren't performing and changing hiring policies to look for creative designers, not just people with degrees.[3]

The brand branched out to piggyback off popular movies like *Star Wars*, comic-book characters like Spider-Man and Batman, and games like *Minecraft*. In 2014 it released its first standalone film, which turned more than $460 million at the box office.[4] New mechanical ranges were developed to hook older kids and, in the digital space, Brickipedia now connects us with our favourite childhood Lego sets. Lego's standalone stores are bright and welcoming, and encourage children to feel and play with real Lego bricks. The company has even released a bioplastic range, showing it cares about the world its customers live in.

And just like that, an old stalwart on the brink of collapse has adapted for a new age.

The lesson is in: build a business around what consumers want before they tell you exactly what that is by shopping elsewhere.

MAKING CONNECTIONS

China – currently the world's second-largest economy and looking to improve on that position – has been playing a pivotal role in the global revolution for years.[5] In 1979, the Chinese government enforced the 'one child policy', which restricted parents to having only one child. Although the law was relaxed in 2013[6], it has been a driving force behind robotics and gaming in the country, two industries seemingly designed to keep lonely children busy.

Loneliness isn't reserved for Chinese children. The creation of AI-powered adult companions is proof that people want a more realistic connection to address their need for friendship and entertainment. AI might be in its infancy, but the age of building and ordering friends that very closely resemble human counterparts is approaching.

With Facebook use in decline among younger users[7], and social networks in general moving away from connecting with friends towards self-published broadcasting, I believe the consumers of the future will expect brands to add value to their life with experiences and technology that re-create human connection.

This doesn't mean you need to transform your business into a tech start-up; it means you need to use technology to create a business that gives people the choice to connect with other humans.

4 STEPS TO ELEGANCE

Here are my four steps to help you ensure elegance in everything you do, without upsetting the harmony or balance that's at the heart of your business.

1 Shift from communication to connection

As outlined here, when brands connect with people in a real way, they create solutions that make a difference in their lives. Companies like UberPool and the co-working and co-living subscription service Roam are good examples of early efforts to prioritise that connection.

To get to that point, as a person or as a business, means you need to stop talking and start *listening*. What people say reveals their needs and pain points – and opportunities.

2 Stop selling, start positioning

You might be a business owner, but you're also a consumer, and that means brands are always trying to sell you something. Annoying, right?

Instead of trying to turn everything into sales, focus on giving your customers what they want. Initially, this will be at low or no cost. Instead of pushing product on your social pages, connect with your customers as a brand. Draw consumers in by building trust over time instead of ramming your reality down their throat. Once you become a trusted adviser, you'll have a solid foundation for sustained, elegant solutions that will convert goodwill into sales – when the customer is ready.

3 Understand that training isn't education

Employees who are educated, rather than trained, are the hallmark of elegant business. Teaching people how to follow processes is the same as programming robots. Rather, equip your workforce with the knowledge they need to face any challenge and deliver a consistent experience.

Training only tells people *how* to do something. When we're educated, we know *why* we do things, and that bigger picture is a source of motivation in itself.

4 Realise that significance is the new success

Success as we know it today comes and goes; significance lasts forever. We need to change the way we measure success, moving away from fussing over marginal profits to solving real-world problems: from making cents to making sense. (See SHOTs 8 and 20.)

In a hyper-transparent and connected world, a focus on significance is the route to long-term profitability. Concentrating on solutions that have positive consequences in a changing world will lead to elegant connections and help you see those invisible dots more clearly than ever before.

THE BOTTOM LINE

In an increasingly complex and confusing world, elegant solutions are becoming the basis of long-term success, while success itself is being redefined. Cult brands have shown us beautifully simple ideas that we can *experience* and will change the way we live our lives, and mainstream brands that want to survive in the long term are starting to heed these examples. Consumers aren't just being put first, they are being involved in the way the company operates – along with employees, who are more valued than in days past.

It's time to learn the fundamentals of doing elegant business, connecting humans in the process.

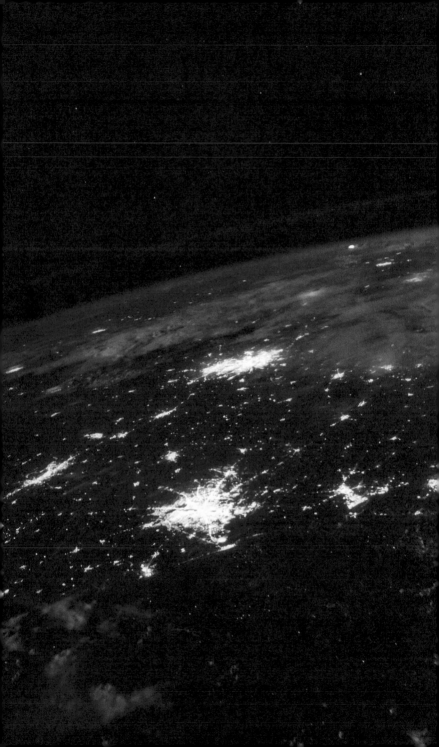

AN ADAPTABLE ATTITUDE

WHAT WE NEED TO TEACH OUR KIDS

Expectation *n* a decision to suffer if things don't go exactly as we planned[1]

I'll never forget a trip I took to St Petersburg in Russia in early 2017. On the way back, we got stuck on the runway for seven hours, waiting for the engines to thaw. It was -22°C outside.

The delay had some 'interesting' effects on my fellow passengers. One lady, a mother with four children, lost her temper. I'll give her her due; she deserves an Olympic gold for making that trip on her own with four children. But she didn't realise how embarrassed her kids were. Or what her antics were teaching them in the process.

I think everyone else was embarrassed for them too. Russia is a powerful nation, but there's nothing it can do about its weather.

Most of us are like that rigid mom: stuck to our schedule and bound to suffer (anger, sadness, horror, you name it) when things don't go according to plan. But that's exactly the wrong kind of attitude to have in a future where life as we know it is changing. Surprises will become more and more common in our fast-evolving world – including unpredictable weather extremes, by the way – and those who are triggered the least by the unexpected will be more successful in the game of life.

A point of clarification

There's a critical difference between being ready to adapt and 'going with the flow'. The former, what we're talking about in this SHOT, comes in the context of knowing your purpose and end goals, and is one of the keys to thriving today. The latter lacks long-term intention and may as well be 'floating along with no direction'; a route to nowhere or anywhere and, despite its 'chilled' connotations, a generator of anxiety because it leaves everything to fate and deprives us of the opportunity to create our own future. Being adaptable doesn't mean you're so relaxed, you're almost horizontal. It means that you are able to alter your course when needed, as you sail with purpose to your destination.

AUGMENTED ADAPTABILITY

By applying certain shifts in perspective in our life, it becomes easier for us to see patterns, adapt to a changing environment and avoid collapsing into an exhausted, exasperated mom of four every time we face an unexpected challenge. These shifts also help us discard the perspectives that are holding us back.

The first step is to replace being *expectant* with being *acceptant*. By its very nature, expectation is rooted in HINDsight and PLAINsight – but, as we know, the past and the present hold no guarantees for the future. Instead of expecting things to go exactly as planned, accept that they won't; by doing so, you'll be able to approach every moment with less anxiety. Nothing can go 'wrong' when you're not expecting a single fixed set of outcomes.

Next, we need to revisit our definition of gratitude and allow ourselves to be fascinated by life. When something fascinates us, we are automatically grateful, which is far more meaningful than just saying 'thank you' and settling for a life that doesn't excite or inspire. When we are ready to adapt, we come to see uncertainty as fascinating, rather than frightening. As Joe Dispenza says, 'the unknown has never let me down'.[2]

One consequence of choosing to be fascinated is that we become absolutely obsessed, rather than merely interested or even passionate. Passion is important but it has become standard; we need to live a new normal where we find a healthy source of obsession, and let it drive our every decision.

To ensure we don't create unhealthy obsessions, though, we need to understand why we're pursuing a goal. Acting out of fear and desperation will drive us to dangerous places, but if we run towards something because we love it, we will be fuelled by perpetual inspiration.

My friend Steve Uria offers a perfect example. Two decades ago he became obsessed with changing the fitness space from his base in New York, and he's been doing exactly that ever since. He's now a renowned physical trainer working on a global scale. Building his empire is his way of life; training like a machine is his normal. (He's literally running towards something he loves.) I am inspired by his drive because, just like him, I am also absolutely obsessed with what I do.

Making these shifts isn't something we actively learn to do. As outlined earlier, preparing our perspectives is about *unlearning* – in this case, unlearning what we know about expectation and gratitude. It's not easy to prepare for the impossible, but in the new world it is essential. And it applies particularly to our children. We're making a tomorrow for today's children, and we need them to be adaptable enough to revel in it.

Once, Intelligence Quotient was the full measure of an individual; a child's IQ was all-important. Then we came to understand the importance of Emotional Quotient; we had to encourage EQ too. Today, the third piece of the pie is Adaptability Quotient; work on that AQ.[3] The Boy Scout motto 'Be Prepared' has taken on new meaning.

THE OBSESSION AND GRIT OF TOMORROW'S LEADERS

Not too long ago, it was common for children as young as six to be sent off to traditional boarding schools to study an established set of subjects. It was the plan. (See SHOT 4.) Happily, that doesn't happen as much any more.

Like so many industries, education is undergoing transformative disruption. We've touched on the crisis at universities, but the revolution extends from the earliest preschool classes to the highest echelons of tertiary education. Of course, the curriculum is changing: kids now learn how to code instead of conjugating Latin verbs, and get taught geography with VR and do homework on iPads, and changing cultural norms mean corporal punishment has been replaced by compulsory meditation. But the critical shift will be the one away from teaching a set of processes towards building a framework for flexibility.

I'm not a parent yet (although I've been honoured to be a dog dad), but I can imagine how terrified I'd be by the prospect of my kids' future in a hotter world run by robots. To make sure our children thrive, we need to equip them with a future-proof way of doing things – and it won't hurt the grown-ups to embrace these, either.

First, we have to allow and encourage children to follow their passion.

AI is quickly taking over the logistics-, language- and process-driven functions that our traditional left-brain education system prepared us for, so the next generation must focus on what makes them excited. They'll have to: they are the ones who will have the means, the time and the tools to overcome challenges we can't even comprehend right now.

Passion (obsessions!) and curiosity are playmates, and being curious is a skill all children have in abundance. It's what makes them draw on walls and put their fingers in plug points. Unfortunately, that curiosity is systematically dulled while they learn the same lessons their grandparents did. Keep your kids curious about the world beyond textbooks, and help them master the art of asking questions. (All those questions might drive you nuts. My advice: adapt!)

Second, we must give them the gift of grit and resilience.

Moving from today to the future we're writing won't be easy. Unless you've been raised to embrace ideas with an elastic mind – and even if you have – you're going to face obstacles and doubt. There's no easy way for any of us to instantly become enlightened. That's why it's important to give children the gift of grit and resilience, to make sure they're relentless in the pursuit of their passion. They must be able to push on when success seems far off and get back up when they fall down. Even in this viral age, overnight success is a rarity – a point that struck home for me when I worked out that it took me close to a decade to build critical momentum in my current career.

THE BOTTOM LINE

Famous American author and philosopher Ralph Waldo Emerson is credited with a quote I love, one that's been recycled by politicians and punk rockers alike: 'Your actions speak so loudly, I cannot hear a word you are saying.' It's an observation that could have negative or positive connotations; either way, it remains incredibly relevant. Which is to say, the best way to teach your children has always been to inspire and lead by example – and never has that rule applied more than today, when you need to be a role model for the reality your kids will face. You can't expect them to be passionate, flexible, curious and resilient if you're trapped in a life of memories and missed opportunity. As conscious parenting expert Shefali Tsabary explains it, parents need to evolve so their children can be liberated.[4] *You* have to increase your AQ and start adapting today – cultivating your own passion and curiosity and altering your perspective – so that *they* can thrive tomorrow. If your children inherit adaptability, they will be free to be individuals rather than factory robots on autopilot.

[*11*]

CONNECTED
TO THE BEST

THE IMPORTANCE OF SPECIALISTS IN
A WORLD FILLED WITH JACKS-OF-ALL-TRADES

We're all hybrid humans, forced to wear many hats to keep our businesses competitive. We have to be. As we've seen, it's about adaptability and flexibility.

Not long ago, most companies specialised in one thing. You wouldn't buy fish at a steakhouse, just as you couldn't buy groceries at a petrol station. And that was okay; it meant every business had a clearly defined role to play, market to focus on and ways to meet its targets. Businesses knew *exactly* who their consumers were, often by name.

Our ingrained manufacturing mind-set was still motivating us to think according to Adam Smith's divisions of labour and Henry Ford's production lines. We were stuck on the idea that we had to put a number of people, each specialising in one thing, in sequence to produce anything efficiently. It didn't matter whether they were working on a car or a camera: they repeated a single task, then handed the process over to the next person in line.

The benefits of this were that you could become really good at the one thing you had to do, and the business could become super-efficient by stringing together experts along the entire production process.

The drawback? Technology can replace the human component along most of this production line, performing the tasks more quickly and affordably.

As we entered the new technological age, the sensible reaction to the risks associated with being a specialist was to pick up a number of skills instead of putting all your eggs in one basket. Insurance is increasingly valued in an age of instant redundancy, when the factory worker, switchboard operator and tennis let-call judge have all lost their jobs to sensors and binary code.

That's why so many small business owners today run their own social media accounts, do online courses in design, and try to develop start-ups on the side. The thinking is that it's safer and, in the long run, cheaper to have a set of skills to fall back on if you can't pursue your primary passion.

Employees do it too. I'm sure you've met someone from the 'slash' group: the model/deejay/dog-walker and the designer/dancer/doctor-in-training who also waits tables on weekends.

There is obvious value in working with people of many talents, not least because you can learn from them. But when it comes to business, our preferences seem to be swinging back to specialists – because working with people who have only a vague idea of your goal dilutes the clarity you need to achieve it. After all, you wouldn't entrust your dental health to someone who dabbles in dentistry or let an architect with 'an interest in finance' oversee your investment portfolio. (Seriously, please don't.)

When we become specialists, we naturally tend to seek out people who display the same obsessive excitement about what they do. We team up with other experts, instead of relying on 'kinda can' people.

Once my own purpose and goals had become clear, I sought out the best collaborators, and entrusted my brand to them. Because they were excited about my ideas and the future, they gave me their full attention. They inspired me and gave me the freedom to connect my invisible dots as they connected theirs.

IT'S ALL IN THE DETAILS

Working with experts gives you a chance to tap into the genius of a circle that wants you to succeed.

Take Carla, for example. Carla is a mindfulness coach, although that's like calling the *Queen Mary 2* a boat. She's not a part-time psychic who dabbles in helping others; she is a specialist who has allowed me to understand who I want to become. Her focus is my future and what it's going to take to get me there, and she has helped me find the confidence to head into that future more fluidly and elegantly by bringing more details to my intentions.

One of the most profound exercises she has done with me was a visualisation where I clearly identified my goals. During the session, I told her I wanted to write a *New York Times* bestseller and share a stage with Simon Sinek and other renowned speakers.

She listened, then asked for more details about the vision. What did it feel like to achieve my goal? Where was Sinek standing during my presentation? Was I nervous to be in front of my biggest audience ever?

The exercise helped me to live the moment and use it to fuel my journey towards it. It also highlighted how important the details are when we're constructing our own reality.

Another thing I learnt from Carla is that once you have clarity of purpose, the specialists you need will be attracted into your circle. Like you, they will want to work with someone whose energy flow matches theirs. So be patient when you're looking for the experts who'll help you reach your goals. Draw them in by inspiring them to connect with your genius, and taking them closer to theirs.

THE BOTTOM LINE

When you're forging your future, vague notions and sometimes-maybes don't cut it any more. You need to use the power of perspective to identify what you want to achieve, and then surround yourself with specialists who are able to share your vision and so help you get there. You're a genius, and by attracting other geniuses into your circle, the life you want will happen *through* you, not *to* you.

giving
and
taking

Why both are equally important
in creating opportunities

[*12*]

If you use LinkedIn frequently or you've had a meeting with a digital marketer in the last five years, you've probably heard of Gary Vee and Simon Sinek (the guy I just mentioned). But just in case you haven't, here's a little about them.

Gary Vee (Vaynerchuk) is a brash, fast-talking entrepreneur and digital media specialist. After transforming his family-owned liquor store into a $60-million-a-year e-commerce-linked wine business, he founded VaynerX and the full-service digital agency VaynerMedia. His strategy centres around the concept of 'hustle', and he frequently posts motivational videos about his ideas.

Simon Sinek is a business strategist and organisational consultant who focuses on the psychology that underlies successful business and their owners. He is best known for the concept of 'starting with why' – the subject of a book and a wildly popular 2009 TED Talk[1] – and of using purpose to define your business path. His approach and strategy tend to be more contemplative.

Despite their different delivery styles, Vaynerchuk and Sinek's thinking often syncs up – so much so that they release videos together. The specific video that inspired me recently was all about giving employees more than you take from them.

GIVING AND GETTING

Right off the bat, that's a concept that flies in the face of tradition. Most of us have been brought up to believe that we need to give our all in order to impress our bosses and prove our worth. It's one of the reasons we work ourselves to death.

This expectation is shared by our bosses, who are used to taking everything from their employees and giving back only the bare minimum, whether in terms of salary, days off, mentorship, or just a bit of slack for a worker going through a tough time.

In the video[2], Sinek explains how he uses an exercise called 'Give and Take' to find out what his potential colleagues and partners can give to his business, and what they want to take from him.

Picture it: you're sweating your way through an interview, and your interviewer asks you what you can offer. You list all your skills, just like you prepared. But how do you answer when he flips the script and asks what you're going to *take* from the opportunity?

'Um... inspiration?'

That's not what Sinek is after. He wants to know what people want to take selfishly from him. In other words, what do you want Simon Sinek to give you in exchange for the skills you provide?

This is more than a pressure test. It's a construct for people to prove that they're both selfless and ready to give, *and* that they're also selfish enough to take – and in what proportion.

If what people can give is on par with what they're going to take, you end up in a balanced relationship. Working through imbalanced relationships, as so many people do, leads to resentment and complaints about money, work satisfaction, fulfilment and that awful boss of yours.

Gary Vee has a different approach to balance, which he calls 51:49 – the ratio needed to overdeliver (ever so slightly) without tilting the balance of a relationship to a point where value is no longer fairly exchanged. It's designed to make him look good.

He is open about his ulterior motive: leverage. His employees and partners are satisfied because they're getting more than they expect – so they're more likely to stay, and mirror the attempt to overdeliver.

This strategy might not feel as warm and fuzzy as Sinek's, but the fact remains that Gary Vee still gives more than he takes. And that got me thinking about the attitude we need to develop in order to forge an abundant future.

WE'RE NOT WORTHY

When I was collecting the many testimonials and documents that I'd need for my planned move to

New York – not easy when you're a South African of Iranian descent – I asked my friend Yossi for help. The process involved me sending countless emails and messages that started with, 'Sorry to bother you but...' Like most people would, I kept apologising for putting him out. I had immediately assumed that helping me would be an inconvenience for him.

We've all been there: we ask for assistance or advice, and then we say sorry a thousand times when we get it.

Then Yossi said something that changed everything for me, right down to the way I breathe. (Really.) He said that while I kept apologising, I was effectively resisting his efforts to give me something and so denying him the opportunity to be generous.

Whoa.

I hadn't thought about the situation from his perspective. Once I did, I realised I was being strangely selfish (to my detriment). I wasn't allowing him to be generous because something inside me didn't think I was worthy of that generosity.

Here's another example. A friend of mine once offered to make me an on-the-spot lunch. I was hungry, but I didn't want her to go out of her way, so I told her no thanks, I was okay. Happily, she persisted, I caved, and she made me an unbelievable meal. At the time, I felt weird about being cooked for, because I wasn't ready to receive her generosity.

She, on the other hand, was confident about giving, and that by doing it she would take something in return – my gratefulness, the pleasure in doing a friend a good turn.

It's not just about offers of help. We struggle to accept things – compliments, advice, gifts – because we don't think we're worthy of receiving these things. It seems that, for many of us, loving is easy, but being loved is a skill we need to practise.

It's essential that we modify this mind-set.

> THE ONLY WAY WE'LL BE ABLE
> TO EXPECT, CREATE AND ALLOW
> INTO OUR LIVES A NEW FUTURE IS
> BY RECEIVING THE LESSONS, ADVICE
> AND LOVE THAT PEOPLE ARE SO
> FIERCELY TRYING TO GIVE US.

Receivership starts with saying, 'I'm worthy'. It's connected to the idea of self-compassion (which we'll look at in more detail in SHOT 14). Once we are healed and no longer held back by painful memories, we are ready to receive gratitude and gifts from others, and to share our gifts more freely in turn.

Practising receivership starts with preparing our bodies. Following my mind-opening conversation with Yossi, I started by focusing on every breath that

I receive, feeling it deep in my solar plexus. It's a simple exercise, but it helps prepare me to receive whatever the world wants to give me.

‖‖  ‖‖‖

THE BOTTOM LINE

What we get in life is directly proportional to how worthy we think we are. How much you forgive and love yourself will define your world and what happens through you. We can never take advantage of the opportunities on offer tomorrow if we're not ready to receive them, whether at work or in our personal relationships. Stop denying yourself: you are worthy of everything that you can receive, today and in the future. Now, it's time to give *and* receive.

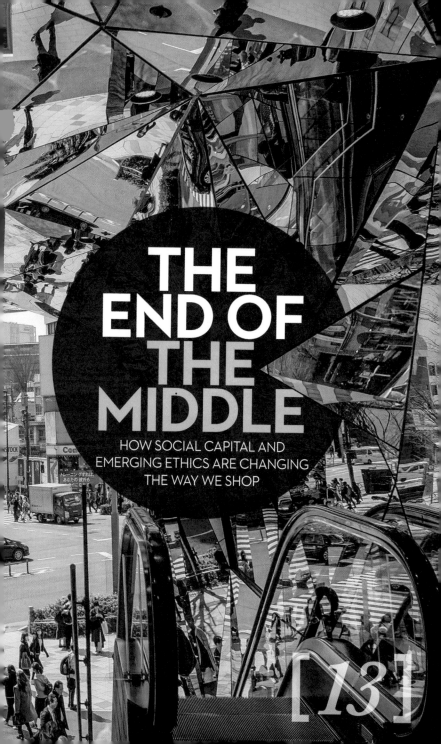

THE
END OF
THE
MIDDLE

HOW SOCIAL CAPITAL AND
EMERGING ETHICS ARE CHANGING
THE WAY WE SHOP

[13]

If you've ever looked at all the receipts stuffed into your pocket, you may have noticed that we spend most of our shopping budget on everyday goods: groceries and daily consumables. Getting these things usually involves a trip to a supermarket, possibly a mall, after work or on the weekend – which is a pain. It's called 'convenience shopping' but it's only convenient in comparison to how we shopped in days of yore, waiting weeks for our provisions to arrive at the general store.

Over time, we've upgraded from general stores and country markets to supermarkets and malls, and now we're upgrading to the net. As online shopping starts to take over, commentators everywhere are predicting the approaching retail apocalypse. But I believe we're at the starting point of a new global culture that's not just going to change the way we shop; it will change our lives.

WELCOME TO THE END OF THE MIDDLE

The retail sector, a term I use broadly for the shopping industry, mirrors our society's division between the industrial and innovation mind-set. On one side, we have automatic, 'industrial' shopping: struggling for parking, shuffling through crowded shops, waiting to pay at the end of it, all for things we can get in any supermarket. There's nothing memorable or exciting about this simple machine: money in, stuff out. You don't even need a human teller.

Shopping online follows the same model – browse and buy – but minus the car trip, crowds and queues, which saves a lot of time and effort. The fact that you can buy everything from makeup to cars online indicates how innovative brands have capitalised on our demand for (genuine) convenience.

Meanwhile, some companies are actively connecting the two models. Amazon Go lets you walk into a store, load your basket and leave. An app linked to dozens of cameras tracks what you pick up, and you're billed as you take things off the shelf – no more standing in line at a cashier. Amazon has also tested Dash, small buttons for specific items at home that you would press to reorder when you were running low. It's already out of date; Alexa and automatic reordering are replacing it.

Then there's Alibaba's Hema store franchise in China. Visitors shop via an app, scanning barcodes and paying for groceries on the spot, and have the option of building shopping lists and profiles of regular purchases that can be ordered for delivery next time around.

The varying solutions these companies are offering may look the same – digitally driven responses to meet consumer needs – but the difference between innovation and disruption quickly becomes apparent. On one hand, Amazon and Alibaba are using technology to make the existing experience faster and less of a hassle; on the other they are making the transition to predictive ordering based on customers' needs, an entirely new form of retail. This ability will only get more advanced as the Internet of Things makes our data profiles so rich that brands can start reacting to our needs before we acknowledge them.

Suggestion metrics are algorithms that analyse information like average spend, purchase frequency and what we're buying to build data profiles that can be used to predict what we'll want and when – because what we buy tells stories about who we are. Buying nappies every week? You're a parent. Bought golf clubs and tees over the past few weeks? Wannabe Tiger Woods. No meat on the menu? Probably vegetarian.

This data profile will become increasingly clear as we interact with new technology around the home. Smart fridges will be able to sense when we're running low on nut milk and veggies, and order more. Smart TVs will pick up that we watch family films on Netflix every Friday, and make sure we're stocked with popcorn and wine gums.

It runs deeper than that. Broadcasting a traumatic event like a break-up could trigger a flower delivery.

You might watch a video on how to cook a recipe and have the ingredients delivered to make it as you watch. Always listen to a specific song when you're sad? Your significant other could get an alert and order something to cheer you up.

Once we start living lives where we are connected to the brands that supply us, and our data profiles become detailed enough, retailers won't wait for us to decide what we need – they'll work it out for us and send it over.

FOR SALE: EXPERIENCES

Experience shopping is that little bit of shopping that we actually enjoy; the shopping that retailers try to prolong rather than speed up. Brands operating in this space have an understanding of two key concepts: our need for communal connection and for entertainment.

The local weekend farmers' market is a chance to spend your money on fresh stuff and great food, but also to meet people: the farmer selling organic apples, the small start-up team selling Fairtrade coffee. It's a far more appealing, human experience than the supermarket – and big brands are taking note.

Nike recently opened a concept store that doubles up as a community space. The global hotel network

Ibis has transformed its positioning to encourage a sense of shared space and connection. 3Den in New York is a co-working community designed around bringing people together, complete with spa, yoga studio, standing desks and sleep pods.

Visiting these spaces isn't about just buying sneakers or enjoying a service – it's an experience in itself, and you get to connect with like-minded consumers who hunt down the cool, too. It's also a way to boost your social score, which brands are increasingly aware of.

Going social

Back in the day, the brands we wore were a badge. We boasted with little logos (that got progressively bigger), which reflected our social status at malls and parties. Today social media has revolutionised this process. Now it's not just your immediate circle who sees what you're wearing and what you're doing; you can broadcast your image to half a billion active daily users on Instagram alone.[1] And it's becoming less about boasting about a brand – endorsing corporate culture is falling out of favour – and more about sharing experiences and movements to build social capital.

But posting pictures of the salad you're having for lunch or a blurry party video doesn't cut it; for something to be worthy of the Gram, it needs to be unique. The more out of the ordinary or fringe, the better – preferably something with a deeper moral purpose.

Social media has become the obvious space for innovative retailers to operate – but it is a complex and fast-shifting space. Some of the moves seem standard; for instance, employing armies of influencers, from local tweens who are given free stuff to promote, to the big leagues where Kylie Jenner gets paid $1 million for sponsored Instagram posts.[2] But brands need to be careful to position themselves, not oversell (see p115/SHOT 9), as they make retail experiential.

Get it wrong and there can be serious blowback. Various Kardashians have taken heat for endorsing products in a way that seems forced and inauthentic: for instance, pushing weight-loss products without mentioning the role their personal trainers, nutritionists and surgeons may have played in helping them to slim down.[3] The Kardashians will always survive; the products perhaps not.

Modern consumers want real human connection, which they can then choose to broadcast themselves if it adds to their social clout. Brands need to be able to deliver both: a chance to be part of a community that's unique, and matching experiences that are dramatic enough to enhance social capital.

NEXT CUSTOMER PLEASE

Brands that haven't been able to meet the audience's appetite for experiences and connection are really up against it.

Clothing giant The Gap is scheduled to close 230 locations in the next two years.[4] Similarly, JC Penny is due to close 19 stores in 2019. Kraft Heinz, one of the biggest names in food, lost $12.6 billion in 2018, and will lose more in 2019 (with related stock-price plunges).[5] Campbell US, the soup that inspired Andy Warhol, has been in decline for four years.[6]

Compare this with brands that have embraced the consumers' need for experience and built businesses around pain points.

Meal-kit service Blue Apron fused convenience with fun, delivering ingredient-and-recipe meal kits, valued at $2 billion in three years.[7]

Domino's is effectively a tech brand that sells pizza, creating loyalty through tech innovation that allows you to order on social media using the pizza emoji. Even though you may think Domino's pizza is average to bad, the company's stock has soared since 2010, outperforming Amazon and the other tech giants[8], and that's because they're tapped into the pulse of what people expect from brands today – which includes predicting and recommending what we might want, and then getting it to us as effortlessly as possible.

In a different industry but similar vein, Spotify is an amazing example of a company that can tell its customers what they didn't know they wanted. Personally, Spotify has introduced me to worlds of music that I would never have found alone. Netflix does the same; the way you watch and what you choose plays a big role in what they recommend you binge next – and how often do they get it right? Almost always.

THE BOTTOM LINE

Selling products and services is yesterday's business. Although there will always be a market for certain products and services, commodities will be disrupted first and frequently. The new customer looks for social capital in other ways.

Selling memorable experiences is today's business, and brands that are offering that to their consumers are winning right now. That said, I believe that the customer-experience approach will also become commoditised and markets will become savvy to it.

The next evolution, then, is the creation of brands that offer a genuine connection based on our values. Within that world, business is far less about products and profits, or even building experience platforms that boost consumers' online profiles. This is an opportunity to stand for a cause, and attract people to your business based on morals and values.

That man Elon Musk, as controversial as he may be, is a shining example of this. Interested in reducing your carbon footprint? Buy a Tesla. Worried about our planet's future? Follow SpaceX. Unsure about humanity's future in the face of exponential tech? Check out Neuralink.

Musk must still contend with the challenges and doubters that come with the old way of thinking, but I back him to succeed in the long run. He has created brands that people support because their values and concerns resonate and align – and that's what cult brands do. They go beyond the norm and redefine our expectations of what brands are. They focus on the long game, turning moral momentum into social movements – and that's the business of the future.

SHOT 13 **THE END OF THE MIDDLE**

[*14*]

THE MYTH OF
SELF-ESTEEM

WHY SELF-COMPASSION IS
THE SMARTER ROUTE TO SUCCESS

I find it really amusing when I meet someone and can clearly see who they're pretending to be. They borrow jokes from their favourite comedian, their style from an actor, their philosophy from whatever social media influencer they're following at the time.

We're all monsters of Frankenstein, made up of fragments of the characters we want to be. In some ways this is inevitable. Like artists, we're influenced by the people we meet and the ideas we encounter; we keep what we want and let go of what we don't. That's how we build our self-image, and from there the self-esteem that is the bedrock of our wellbeing...

Spoiler alert.

Self-esteem is *not* the bedrock of your wellbeing. It is not the miracle solution to all your problems. Trust me – I've learnt the hard way.

I spent nearly 40 years chasing the success I thought I needed to become what I thought other people thought I should be. (Try saying that three times fast!) It took me all that time to realise that my reliance on self-esteem, in order to protect my self-image, was preventing me from accepting who I really was. And until I accepted *that* person, the real John Sanei, I could never forge the best way forward for me.

#SELFFIRST

Why do we yearn so deeply to be things we are not? Why do we try so hard to protect our façade of self-image? Why do we put ourselves through cycles of aspiration and disappointment?

Modern news-media culture in general, and social media in particular, have certainly exacerbated this problem. You can't pick up your phone without seeing someone living the life you think you want. You can't walk past a magazine stand without an aspirational cover line (effectively) telling you you're not good enough. It's so much easier (in the short run) to pretend you're the person in your Instagram profile than it is to develop your personality.

Mostly, though, we do it because that's how we've always done it.

We're born to find and follow role models. Older siblings, parents and teachers are there to guide us with what worked for them – so we learn from HINDsight. In time, we replace them with celebrities, musicians and friends who seem to be living the lives we long for – so we learn from PLAINsight.

At some point we stop learning. We don't try to understand whether the success we see is real or just an elaborate act. We copy and paste what we want to hear, inheriting the advice and prejudices of others. And then we bludgeon ourselves into thinking we're on the right track with self-esteem, that trendy trait that tells us to *believe* in ourselves at the cost of actually *knowing* ourselves.

> SELF-IMAGE AND SELF-ESTEEM ARE DANGEROUS ILLUSIONS. WE DON'T NEED SELF-IMAGE; WE NEED GENUINE IDENTITY. WHICH MEANS WE DON'T NEED SELF-ESTEEM; WE NEED THE SELF-COMPASSION THAT WILL ALLOW US TO CREATE OUR IDENTITY FROM THE INSIDE OUT.

Our self-esteem depends on how we think we're perceived. It's a fire fuelled by Instagram followers and Facebook likes, compliments and congratulations from people who put us on a pedestal and reinforce that what we're doing and how we're being is right. Ultimately, this means we spend our lives waiting for someone else to tell us we're geniuses instead of just realising we are geniuses and getting on with it.

Self-compassion is about looking inwards, healing our heart, and becoming comfortable with who we really are, no matter who that person is.[1] When you truly care about the real you, you put yourself in charge of the world around you, rather than being a victim of that world.[2]

This isn't about being selfish; it's the opposite. Being compassionate towards ourselves creates an environment in which we can start sharing that compassion with others, and that attracts the right people and opportunity into our lives. (Bonus: when you start helping others and sharing your gifts with them, you in turn will feel loved.)

Self-compassion helps us prepare to become future-fluid, because when we care about ourselves we don't beat ourselves up when things change, and we don't allow anxiety to control us.

MAKING THE CHANGE

The motivation to create a new identity based on self-compassion rather than self-esteem is a compelling one. But we have to be disciplined and prepared to allow our perspective to change. For this process, I suggest using three invisible containers to hold the new energy and intentions you require, and to ensure you maintain your discipline throughout.

Because the containers are clear, you can always see what's inside each one – and remove what shouldn't be. They have defined boundaries, so you can categorise lessons and make decisions about your future with conviction. And they don't leak, so you don't lose power through indecision and ill-discipline; instead, you channel everything you've got into your own life.

Container 1: Your emotions

You can't create a future without a clean slate. Start with your heart. Heal yourself so you can move on; deal with bitterness, resentment and blame; and break ties with or forgive the people who've held power over you (which you have allowed). This is not a process to take lightly, but its value is profound.[3] (See SHOT 6.) Look into your emotional container often to see how you're doing. It's important that there are no cracks in the container; our emotions can be tricky to control, and when they leak they trigger uncertainty, fear and doubt.

Container 2: Your physical body

To love and respect yourself, you need to look after the physical vessel that carries you through the incredible adventure of life. You also need to be physically ready to follow any path. That means taking care of your body.

Drawing inspiration from Steve Uria (the man who taught me the difference between mere motivation and life-changing discipline; we met him in SHOT 10), I made a commitment to get into the best shape of my life. I focused on my pH levels, the microbiotics in my stomach, the probiotics I get from kombucha, kefir, kimchi and other fermented food – and I did, and still do, five kickass workouts a week, no matter what.

I train not because I hate my body and need to punish it, but because I love and respect it. This is the container that helps create firm walls and seals for the other two containers.

Container 3: Your mind

The third container is the one that will keep your thoughts on track; the one that prevents you from chasing counterproductive self-esteem; the one that prioritises FOREsight over the other sights. Fill this container with all you need to be mentally prepared for the reality in which you achieve your goals: flexible, strong, high-performance thinking.

‖‖‖ ‖‖‖

THE BOTTOM LINE

We are not carbon copies of the people we've observed in the past or admire today. We are all geniuses with unique gifts and talents to connect invisible dots to somewhere – but you can only discover where exactly when you understand your true identity. Be wary of self-esteem: don't push yourself to be something you're not. Instead, embrace self-compassion: learn who you are and allow yourself to make mistakes in becoming the best possible version of that person.

FUTURE FOOD

WHY FOOD ENTREPRENEURS,
NOT ANGRY VEGANS, WILL CHANGE
THE WAY THE WORLD EATS

I am a plant-based human, not because it makes for a trendy Instagram bio, but because I believe it's better for my health and kinder to the animals we share the planet with. I'm not a door-to-door salesman for this lifestyle, but we've all seen how they operate, and I find it fascinating to watch the especially militant vegans bite off more than they can chew during online debates.

I often see vegans lambasting (bad choice of words?) people who choose to eat meat. They get so triggered and caught up in their anger that they miss out on a real opportunity to inspire change. And, of course, they don't save any animals because nobody changes their beliefs or habits by being told off.

This anger trap isn't new: we've inherited it because we were raised to believe we need to win at all costs. We're convinced this outlook will help us ensure we make enough money, pair up with a suitable mate, and succeed in the boardroom.

Many of us are addicted to anger and anxiety: it's a habit that defines our identity, and we're afraid to let go of it. This is a direct result of being motivated by safety and security, and the immature masculinity that has been the driver of previous generations. Many of us can't seem to shake the sense that we need to fight for our lives. Thanks, evolution.

Thankfully, the majority of us no longer have to fight for our food, which gives us an opportunity to evolve our views. Lesson number one? Choose peace over victory.

MAKE PEACE, NOT WAR

Extraordinary things become possible when we stop worrying about winning and focus instead on creating a peaceful life. It's an approach I prefer to use with my own team.

Even when I'm working with the best specialists there are occasions when I don't get exactly what I'd asked for on the first try. Sometimes, it's not right the second time, either. That's to be expected, and when it happens I start by being a team-mate and accepting half the responsibility for the work I've been presented. I prefer not to shift the blame or pointlessly assert dominance. Rather, I try to be more careful in explaining what I had originally wanted and ensuring we work as closely together as needed to get it right.

Moving away from an insistence on victory means I don't divide my world – or team – into winners and losers. In my experience, the more productive environment that attracts the type of people I want to work with is a peaceful, calm one. We don't need every interaction to be a binary 'win or lose' result.

This shift can completely change our approach to business. Rather than trying to destroy our competitors, we can share our weapons of peace to fight for the future.

Knowledge sharing, where we willingly exchange information or ideas for the common good, is not new. In 1959, when Swedish engineer Nils Bohlin created the three-point safety belt for Volvo, the car manufacturer didn't hold on to it for profit. It shared it, because it would save more lives that way.[1]

The open-source Linux operating system, first released in 1991, is an early IT example. Today, tech giants like Google release some of their proprietary knowledge for free because they know that, with these tools, people can create, design and produce platforms and solutions that benefit everyone.

Collaboration helps us develop superior products. It keeps us flexible and fluid, because we end up working with experts at the cutting edge of their field – people who prioritise progress over profit.

SO, WHAT'S FOR DINNER?

Feeding eight billion people isn't easy, but it will be impossible if we keep doing things the way our farming forefathers did, or keep using our current processes. To date, all we've done is scale up, moving from subsistence farming to mass production – a change that came about when farmers realised people would pay for the convenience of not having to work the land and square up to the seasons. Our solution to feeding growing communities was to build bigger and more productive farms, and we've never stopped.

According to United Nations stats, about 11% of the Earth's surface is used for farming, and two-thirds of that is used to raise livestock – mostly cows.[2] Cows release enormous amounts of methane which – like carbon dioxide – is a key chemical contributing to man-made climate change.[3] Our demand for fish, chicken and other meat is also higher than sustainable supplies.[4]

What we need now is not angry vegans: what we need is entrepreneurs ready to act on opportunities that will make a difference. And they are.

Companies in this sector are starting to choose peace and are putting profits aside, or making them secondary, to focus on long-term ideas for delivering a sustainable food supply.

We as individuals are also trying to make an impact. In the US alone, veganism has increased by 600% in three years, and the trend is growing across the globe.[5] It's sparked a new economy – 'veganomics' – and it's shifting the way we view the business of food.

Every person who chooses to reduce their meat intake is making a difference, but with climate change accelerating, this is not enough. We need to change the entire food chain.

FOOD 2.0

Richard Branson, the visionary founder of the Virgin brand, has said that in the future he believes we'll be shocked by the methods commonly used to feed humanity right now. He is one of the many high-profile voices who have spoken out on the way we treat the animals we eat. Writers, philosophers, leaders and businesspeople are all seeing that the way we eat must, and will, change. The difference with Branson is he's investing in solutions.[6]

What, then, is the future of food?

To start, the trend towards eating ethically farmed meat, and less of it, will continue. Many shopping aisles give us the option to select and eat sustainable food, which is a signifier that attitudes are shifting, if not the game-changer itself. The giant leaps in the right direction will include commercial insect farms and lab-grown and plant-based meat alternatives.

Although many of us would prefer not to harm any living thing, insects provide an abundant source of food for people and animals alike. Insect farms take up considerably less space, and have a far smaller carbon footprint. Insect-based animal feed is safe for animals[7], and commercial feed is being trialled by McDonald's as the company tries to reduce its reliance on soy protein. It's also trying peas, canola and algae to make a difference.

People gag at the idea of gobbling grubs, but in time new practices become accepted. Similarly, lab-grown meat may sound icky, but as many commentators have observed, it's a lot less icky than feedlots and slaughterhouses. Will eating a locust kebab or a tasty beef burger grown in a petri dish be any different from the first time you tried sushi?

Meanwhile, Burger King has added the Impossible Whopper, a meatless version of its famous burger, to its menu, planning a national roll-out in the US by the end of 2019. Other operators are following suit.

These are just some of the obvious examples. Elsewhere, we can already make molecular 'aged' whiskey in 24 hours.[8] We are 3D-printing food. Some of the world's best restaurants rely on rooftop gardens for fresh produce.

In *Magnetiize* I suggested that drone deliveries may eventually eliminate our need for fridges. In case you missed it, here's my train of thought: thanks to tech advances and new regulations, we will one day replace delivery trucks with efficient, almost-instant drone drops of pretty much anything we need, including groceries. This shift in delivery tech coincides with renewed consumer understanding. The boom of food-delivery businesses and at-home cooking subscriptions like US-based Blue Apron and British Gousto is proof that people are moving past traditional monthly shopping trips that were meant to stock enormous fridge-freezers.

Drones can deliver fresh groceries and drastically cut emissions, and once they're commonplace, we won't need fridges. All we'll need is a cooled dock, so a drone can drop off the fresh food (that an algorithm has ordered on our behalf). If I was in the fridge business, I'd be working on developing those docks.

But what other dots can we connect?

A kitchen without a fridge means extra space. Energy-efficient wall-mounted pans are replacing bulky stoves in homes and restaurants, because most of us only cook in a pan anyway. Again, more space.

What will we do without clunky appliances? Well, we can replace them with vertical veggie gardens – you can't get fresher produce than from your own kitchen – or anything else we fancy: a gym, a remote office or just extra space to relax in.

Architects can design communal kitchens within residential buildings for people to connect, eat and cook together. And that rooftop farm will become an absolute must.

THE BOTTOM LINE

Things are getting crowded on our little planet, and space is becoming an increasingly valuable commodity. If we can save space and do the ethical thing by reducing our farming footprint, we'll be solving several problems at once. We've never faced a scenario like this when it comes to food, but if you apply FOREsight, you'll see that there's a feast of opportunity to be had. Just be sure to present your solutions from a place of peace, not war, and avoid the angry online lectures...

[*16*]

THE POWER OF PROJECTION

THE VALUE OF TURNING ARROGANCE INTO CONFIDENCE

Friendship is an interesting concept. Sometimes when we meet someone new, something tells us, 'I like this human. We're going to do things together.' And so we do.

True friends are our confidants and our barometers. They are our mirrors, the people we bounce our thoughts and ideas off. And while advice from mere acquaintances can be taken with a pinch of salt, real friends who know us well are able to tell us the things we need to hear, even if – perhaps *especially* if – we don't want to hear them.

So when some friends I've known since my restaurateur days told me one day that they felt I had become arrogant, I decided it was time for me to do some soul searching.

Once I got over the initial sting of the assessment, I came to realise this was a problem of perspective. Their take on who I had become was, I believe, based on a misunderstanding of the differences between confidence and arrogance, and between lack of respect and irreverence. Ultimately, it was a take that I believe was coloured by the memories of HINDsight and the limitations of PLAINsight.

I'll be the first to admit that I had been spending less time with this particular group of friends. This wasn't because my feelings or fondness for them had diminished in any way; I was just working my ass off to make the move from food to futurism.

I was travelling almost constantly for work, which meant I couldn't dedicate the same amount of time to my friends – not that I no longer cared for them or felt I was too important for them.

They, however, were viewing our relationship from a place of memory: they remembered back to what our friendship had been like when we spent loads of time at my restaurants, chilling out and living it up. As things changed and they saw me only through the filter of my new work and my online activity, they mistook my persona – which I have learnt to keep as authentic and vulnerable as possible – as false, because that wasn't the guy they remembered. Their memories, and what they believed they were seeing, sealed my fate in their eyes.

It's normal for people to drift apart. We all move and grow at different paces, often into different spaces. But there's a deeper issue at play here, and it relates to the way we perceive other people.

When we feel that somebody isn't showing us kindness – or, rather, that they are not meeting our expectations of who they should be and how they should behave – our reaction is to label that person as arrogant, greedy, immature or something similarly undesirable. But is there anything more arrogant than expecting someone's behaviour to conform to what you dictate in your mind?

Think about modern sprint legend Usain Bolt, a nine-time Olympic gold medallist, multiple world record holder and the fastest man ever to grace the Earth. When he first sprinted into the global consciousness, people were divided about his brash persona and showboating before races. As with boxing great Muhammad Ali a generation before, Bolt displayed great confidence in himself and his abilities, and it seems that this attitude was integral to his success.

There are those who would prefer these sporting giants to downplay their talent, and accuse both of arrogance – yet Bolt is now mentioned in the same breath as Roger Federer as one of the gentlemen of modern sport. To me, that self-assurance and swagger equal confidence, not arrogance. Athletes like Usain Bolt hype themselves up psychologically to tap into the persona they need to succeed – to be the version of themselves that can connect the invisible dots to greatness.

In my opinion, the only real difference between arrogance and confidence is kindness.

When people come across as overly sure of themselves and lacking in kindness, we label them as arrogant. When they're sure of themselves but they show us kindness, we say they're confident. The question boils down to: are they being kind and, importantly, are we perceiving that kindness?

Sadly, my friends equated my absence with unkindness, and so they labelled me as arrogant. I've spent a lot of time in recent years in introspection, getting to know and making peace with my inner self, and I'm confident (not arrogant!) that I'm kinder now than I was. (I am trying to show this to them.)

I'm grateful to my friends for being honest with me about how they felt, but I know the conclusion they came to was more a reflection of the way they were looking at me and their expectations of me than my actual behaviour. I understand the origin of that feeling – which I've experienced myself – and I don't let that type of name-calling get me down.

PROJECTION AND PERCEPTIONS

Once you understand that the difference between confidence and arrogance is the perception of kindness, you can start to cultivate another quality that I think is often misunderstood: irreverence.

Like arrogance, irreverence can leave a bad taste in people's mouths in part because of the way it's defined. Google it and you'll to find an explanation along the lines of 'showing a lack of respect for people or things that are generally taken seriously'.

The problem with that definition is how we determine the consensus on respect. I don't believe we have to treat certain ideas or subjects as serious and sombre just because everyone else does. As far as I'm concerned, that's a recipe for conformity, which inhibits our curiosity and the opportunity to ask bold questions.

Imagine how awful and boring comedy would be if almost everything was too serious to joke about. Or how inhibited our society would be, as it was in the past, if we didn't have the space to question authority and perceived wisdom.

Most of us learn respect from the people around us. We acknowledge the values, attitudes and achievements that impress our parents and teachers. We are taught to respect authority and the systems that keep the world working in a certain way. And this is fine – to a degree.

But the lines of respect are blurry, and they shift over time as society evolves. A blind respect for stubborn personal biases and ingrained cultural mores – doing things because they've always been done that way – is a respect that hinders progress. It stops us from deconstructing our world to find patterns and potential.

I encourage irreverence, because it forces us to look deeper and ask the questions of both ourselves and our businesses that will help us prepare for the future. Many of the most profound ideas and advances in human history would never have happened if we'd had too much respect for the accepted way of doing things, whether it was the invention of the printing press which gave the plebs access to books (shocker!) or modern tech companies defying the accepted dominance of the automobile and hotel industries and even government agencies. If we're all too busy trying to fit in, we'll simply allow opportunities to pass us by.

I hope you've had a chance to watch *Bohemian Rhapsody*, the biopic that's made fans fall in love with Queen all over again. The film brilliantly captures the approach of the band's enigmatic front man Freddie Mercury – and that approach is 100% irreverent. To reach the heights he achieved, he had to know exactly who he was, and he wasn't swayed by what people thought of him. That was his power.

> IRREVERENCE IS WHAT HAPPENS WHEN YOU KNOW YOURSELF, WHERE YOU'RE GOING AND HOW YOU'RE GETTING THERE – A STATE THAT BECOMES A SUPERPOWER IN ITSELF.

In such a state, you don't have the energy to waste engaging in the copy-and-paste opinions of others or tearing people down because of the way you perceive them; you're too busy becoming the best version of yourself and solving problems along the way. You don't have time to critique others, so you start to project less and inspire more. That's when you get to find out what kind of magic (more Queen...) you're ready to bring into the world.

It's a step away from the judgment and insecurities that prevent us from learning, because in reality we can learn from anyone and everyone if we choose to. Even the Trumps and Kardashians of the world possess talents and traits we can learn from – but we often miss the opportunity, instead projecting our prejudices onto them.

THE BOTTOM LINE

When we project negative ideas onto people and situations, we lose our power and agency and the chance to learn. We choose to see the worst rather than the best. We become susceptible to the ideas and opinions of others rather than creating our own.

When we project positive ideas, we see the opposite effect. Arrogance becomes confidence. Lack of respect becomes irreverence. We attract insight and opportunity, and ultimately FOREsight.

It's time to focus on yourself, and to cultivate the qualities you'll need to forge your future, without worrying about the way everyone perceives you.

THE AFRICAN OPPORTUNITY

WHY THE NEGLECTED
CONTINENT WILL RISE AS
A DISRUPTION DESTINATION

I recently heard a new word, which is always exciting: 'splinternet'. It refers to the way certain countries, areas and cultures are cut off from the rest of the (supposedly) worldwide web. Censorship in China, poor or nonexistent data connectivity in parts of Africa, and even superfast fibre in Singapore all affect the way people access the internet.

On one hand, people without global internet aren't distracted by social media or forced to wade through fake news to find some kind of truth in the digital echo chamber. They're too busy figuring out solutions for fighting drought and famine to find out which Disney princess they are. On the other (more telling) hand, they also don't have access to the critical information that could help them find the solutions they desperately need.

This digital division got me thinking about real-world geography and the role it's set to play in business and the world of innovation.

DEEPEST, DARKEST DISRUPTION

I've spent a lot of my working life in Cape Town. You may have heard of it: it's often rated as one of the best places in the world to visit. You'll find it at the bottom of Africa, in the shadow of a table-shaped mountain, overlooking the ocean. You can't miss it.

Apart from a healthy lifestyle and views that refresh my spirit, living in the Mother City has given me access to an outlook that you can't find anywhere else.

There are a lot of misconceptions about Africa, probably because the closest most people get to the continent is by watching movies and wildlife documentaries. Outsiders often view it as a vast wilderness filled with wild animals and Third World villages, as though it's a game reserve or, at most, a single country. The classic CNN weather prediction – 'There'll be rain over Africa' – comes to mind.

Of course, Africa is far more complex than this, a continent made up of 54 countries and countless ethnicities, cultures, needs and desires. Along with some of the warmest and friendliest people on earth, it has abundant natural reserves, with an estimated 30% of the Earth's remaining mineral resources. The bounty it offers includes gold, diamonds, cobalt, uranium, copper, platinum, salt, sugar, hardwood, cocoa and tropical fruit. And those wild animals.[1]

But you can't talk about Africa without pointing out its obvious troubles. For centuries it has been abused, first by colonial forces, and more recently by corrupt new elites who can't resist the lure of instant wealth. Many of the most unequal societies on the planet are found in Africa. And while global extreme poverty has declined precipitously over the last three decades (from 37% to 10%)[2], sub-Saharan Africa is still playing catch-up – the incredible strides taken in Asia remain seemingly out of reach for the time being. Famine, disease and low levels of formal education are enormous obstacles.

What does this all equate to?

Opportunity.

Opportunity to try new things, opportunity to implement game-changing technology, opportunity to change lives and, yes, if you must, opportunity to make plenty of profit.

'From a business perspective, the challenges of working in Africa are rooted in the inability of the developed world's technology, financial and investment companies to understand and adapt to local regulatory and socioeconomic challenges,' explains Alexandre Menage, head of sales in Africa for the international banking software company Temenos.[3] In other words, flexibility and adaptability are critical; which is to say the keys to business success in Africa are the same keys that unlock success in the exponential future. (See SHOTs 4 and 10.)

In Africa, you'll find multimillionaires living one wall away from the poorest of the poor, and digital start-ups working to help rural cattle herders and shepherds. In Africa, today, anything is possible.

AFRICA'S TOMORROW

The increasing need for innovative thinkers has led to a reversal of the ancient migration out of Africa. People are not only coming to the continent to learn emergency medicine or discover farming trends, but to borrow from the booming fintech space.

A leader in the latter sector is M-Pesa, the cellphone-based money transfer and micro-financing service that was launched in Kenya in 2007. Powered by Vodafone, it has grown across the continent and branched out to India, Afghanistan, Romania and Albania. In 2018 it upgraded its capacity to be able to provide a phenomenal 1,200 transactions per second.[4] Other notable payment apps include Nigeria's Flutterwave and the lender JUMO, which originated in Ghana.[5]

Then you'll find Bank Zero, a branchless, app-based South African bank pushing the limits of what a bank can be. Nigerian e-commerce group JUMIA is listed on the New York Stock Exchange. Flare, a Kenya-based emergency solutions app uses data to help emergency services reach people in need. Also in Kenya, I had the opportunity to discuss the future of insurance with Jubilee, and I was struck by how progressive the business is: it offers preventative solutions at the cutting edge of its sector.[5]

There are surprises across the continent. Madagascar has faster internet than Germany,

France and South Korea.[6] The average aircraft age of Ethiopian Airlines, Africa's premier carrier, is just six years, compared to 15 and 16 years for Delta and United, for example.[7] Rwanda, scene of one of the most horrendous genocides in modern history just 25 years ago, is now a tech leader: it has a 'One Laptop Per Child' school programme; the goal of a 2015 government initiative is to produce 100 technology companies valued at more than $50 million by 2030; and it introduced public-transport Wi-Fi in 2019.[8]

Meanwhile, there are pockets of business and tech excellence in Nigeria, Kenya, Ivory Coast and South Africa, surrounded by large markets and supported by adequate, if not excellent, infrastructure.

The topper? Success in Africa is *real* success, the stuff that changes lives – the most powerful motivation to drive us all into an optimistic future. (In short, what I'm talking about in this book.)

Investment in African companies opens the door for more businesses, but it also helps to fight disease and increase the rate of poverty reduction. It provides money to build schools and influence a generation of minds that haven't been tainted by global PLAINsight.

Think about the life of an eight-year-old Malawian girl, living in a village, with access to free, fast internet and decentralised green energy. Think about the exponential changes this could mean for her, her family, her community, her village, her country and her continent.

Africa's children will have access to free internet, free education and free power.[9] They will be the first off-the-grid generation immersed in a new way of working. And they will have the opportunity to thrive as the outdated ways of thinking fall away.

If we think of development as a curve, Africa and many other emerging markets are the ones at the right place in time to take things vertical. The booming technology sectors in India and China are proof: they are growing, innovating and inventing exponentially quicker than the developed world.[10] It's time for Africa to follow suit.

||||||||||||||||||||||||||||||||||||||||||||||||||||||||||||||||| ||||

THE BOTTOM LINE

As the global village becomes ever closer and more connected, Africa stands as a continent of boundless potential, a wealth of markets unencumbered by linear thinking and eager to join the abundant future. Its people are warm and inviting, and urgently looking for game-changing solutions to its many long-standing problems – which makes it a perfect fertile ground for big, adaptable thinkers to harness the tech revolution, make a real impact and change the world.

STOP BEING REALISTIC

LIVE LIKE THE WRITER, DIRECTOR
AND STAR OF YOUR OWN MOVIE

[*18*]

You stand, catching your breath. You beam confidently at your colleagues gathered in the boardroom. Behind you, the final slide of your presentation dares them to ask bold, game-changing questions. Your heart is racing, pumping adrenaline through your veins. You've just pitched an idea you think could change the way your business works. All that's left is for everyone to realise the potential of what you've put on the table...

And then the moment starts to drag. The clock starts to slow, and with it your pulse, and you realise there's a chance not everyone has bought into your plans. You scan the room, and no-one's making eye contact – then you hear it.

'We need to be realistic.'

It's a heartbreaking moment, the business equivalent of 'don't call us, we'll call you'.

That little phrase can deflate even the most defiant among us, unless we understand that it's nothing more than an out-of-office reply from minds on autopilot – minds that are stuck in HINDsight, PLAINsight or INsight.

THE IMPORTANCE OF OVERCOMING FEAR

Being realistic used to be a fundamental requirement for business survival and success. It wasn't enough to conceptualise an idea; you needed technology and data to back you, and it was relatively easy to see what was possible. That's no longer the case.

Not too long ago, no company would have dared to declare it would be flying rockets to the International Space Station and eventually to Mars without a proven track record of successful space flights. Now, when SpaceX reveals plans for rockets that will be able to launch and land themselves, with no human interaction from a pilot, you know it's going to happen sooner rather than later.

Today, nothing is impossible, because innovations in tech have resulted in exponential possibilities. In the futuristic year 2000, Sharp released a phone with a 0.11 megapixel camera.[1] Today, we have 64 megapixel cameras[2] that double as broadcasting platforms, social tools and health and lifestyle trackers – and even make phone calls. If you'd predicted the impact of smartphones back then you would have been criticised for not being realistic.

In the interim, the cycle of change and potential is only speeding up. Every day that goes by redefines what's real, so a kneejerk insistence on 'being realistic' is in itself no longer attached to reality; instead, it puts you on a slippery slope to potential redundancy.

While being realistic starts out in a positive place, as a challenge for us to be as objective and clear as we can be, the downside is that it allows fear into the frame, which inhibits our potential. We feel fear just before we get into a shark-diving cage or jump out of an aeroplane because being realistic about the possible outcomes reveals the risks of a situation – yet not making the bold decision denies you that meaningful experience. Similarly, not making the first move – in business or in life – for fear of failure, denies you the potential for meaningful success. When we're afraid, we look over our shoulder towards the comfort blanket of familiarity, and back to our business booty call: HINDsight.

When people in your business tell you to be realistic, what they're actually saying is don't threaten the comfort zone, just stay in the cycle we all know off by heart (though there's no heart involved): review the data, spy on your competition, maybe change a few colours… and repeat.

That's no longer good business – that's simply a fear of failure. We cling to a past that repeats itself instead of using it as a springboard to create something new, because we're afraid to miss targets or deadlines, or our own definition of success.

REAL SUCCESS LIES BEYOND FEAR.
TO GET AWAY FROM THAT FEAR,
YOU NEED TO REDEFINE FAILURE.

As we saw in SHOT 2, Miki Agrawal, author of *Disrupt-her*, proposes a brilliant counterattack to the fear of failure.[3] It is rooted in language, which is so important for future-ready thinking. Because, as she says, the word 'fail' carries with it negative energy, using 'revelation' instead will ready our mind to try new things. Seeing failures as revelations means that you want to keep trying, because even if you miss the mark this time around, you're learning life-shifting lessons.

Softening the notion of failure is also in keeping with the concept of choosing peace instead of chasing, war-like, after 'victory'. When we're not defined as winners and losers, failure isn't an issue. Everyone develops in some way in the process; some people just learn more than others. For resilient, adaptable people like that, every experiment is win-win.

When we're not afraid to fail, we doubt ourselves less. We become more futuristic, brave, excited to become the absolute best version of ourselves. We don't limit our genius to yesterday's ideas. Why would we, when we have the power to connect invisible dots, and enough AQ to flex our future muscles whenever we want?

READY FOR YOUR CLOSE-UP?

If you're not already excited about taking charge and kicking ass, think about it this way: you are the director, star and writer of your own movie.

Before you sign up for acting lessons, I'm not talking about reciting lines of Shakespeare or putting on a façade so you can pretend to be something you're not. What I'm talking about is the adaptability that will allow you to change when you need to, and the confidence to see the whole world as your stage.

Even though Hollywood is all about heartthrobs and leading ladies, it's the directors who are behind the wheel. They control everything from the overall look of the movie to the way actors deliver lines to the final edit. They are visionary storytellers, and the only ones who know what will happen in the end.

Being the boss carries with it the responsibility of knowing that every choice you make affects the end product. And that's exactly how life works. It means you can take responsibility and make decisions that let you take your life in whichever direction you choose. And once you know where you want to end up, you can define the movie in more detail.

Start with the genre. Most people wouldn't want to live in a gory horror film or an angst-ridden drama. They're likely to choose a rom-com or an underdog story full of inspiring changes and accompanied by an epic soundtrack. Your job in defining your own movie is to choose to surround yourself with people who allow you to live that type of life.

Once you've got the genre down, think about the role you'll play. Are you an extra, living on the fringes of the frame, watching other people play the part you actually want? Do you see yourself in a supporting role, always helping other people excel in the life that you long for? Or do you want to be the star, the Oscar-winning hero who saves the world, gets the girl (or guy), and lives happily ever after – and stars in the sequels? I often see people relegating themselves to being bit players for no good reason; we should all aim to be the lead in our own success story.

After that all that's left is to write and refine the script – again, that's your job. Every day, every moment, every time you let go of HINDsight, look deeper than PLAINsight or put INsights into action, you're writing the script of that story.

‖‖‖ ‖‖‖

THE BOTTOM LINE

Your life isn't a rerun. You don't watch repeats of other people's lives and try to live them again. You are the writer, director and star in your own movie, and the reality you depict is for you to define. It's time to cast off fear and take action – all you have to do is stop 'being realistic'!

19

RISE_
OF:_THE

HUMACHINES

WHAT WE'LL ALWAYS

NEED, EVEN WHEN WE'RE

200-YEAR-OLD CYBORGS

Robotics feels like a shiny new industry, but in reality, we've been indulging our God complex by telling stories and creating beings in our own image for thousands of years.

In Greek mythology, the god of fire Hephaestus is said to have created a bronze man to protect Crete from pirates and invaders. Buddhist scholar Daoxuan wrote about 'precious metal people' who recited holy texts and wept when Buddha Shakyamuni died. Artificial men creep into Daoist writing; Jewish lore speaks of golems; and German philosopher and theologian Albertus Magnus is alleged to have built an automaton in the 12th century.

Today, robots are more than mere science-fiction fodder. Right now, solar-powered robotic wolves are protecting livestock in Japan.[1] Laser-equipped robots are analysing and harvesting apples in New Zealand.[2] A robot that kills microbes in hotel beds using UV-C radiation is for sale courtesy of a US robotics company.[3] Working bionic arms are real, affordable and life-changing – look up the 13-year-old Tilly Lockey on Instagram to have your mind blown.[4]

But somewhere along the way, humanity realised that advancing technologies have created the possibility for these servants to threaten our very existence. In film, robots have evolved from the friendly butler in *The Jetsons* to the omniscient and ominous HAL in *2001: A Space Odyssey* and the terrible Terminators that hunt us through time. Whether you're watching them on Netflix's *Love, Death & Robots* or seeing the latest zoomorphic creature from US robotics company Boston Dynamics doing backflips and opening doors on YouTube, they're everywhere.

And the extra airtime they're getting has reignited the debate on whether or not we'll manage to control our robotic creations, or whether they'll control us.

OUR NEXT LEAP

If you tend to take James Cameron movies too seriously, rest assured that the apocalyptic tipping point, when AI realises it doesn't need us, won't be happening any time soon. Even Elon Musk, famously outspoken about the dangers of sentient technology, has changed his perspective, saying he would rather be optimistic and wrong than pessimistic and right when it comes to predicting the future.[5]

That's not to say we don't need to prepare for it. The reality is, we simply can't compete with the speed of modern computing. IBM's Watson can instantly diagnose diseases better than human doctors, and will eventually predict and even pre-empt an individual's future health problems.[6] Summit, the world's fastest supercomputer, can process 200,000 trillion calculations per second[7], and it's about to be knocked off its super-speedy perch by Intel's Aurora. By the time it's switched on in 2021, Aurora will be able to perform a quintillion calculations a second – or one exaflop – which is five times more than Summit.[8] We can't even comprehend that kind of speed: to reach a performance level of a quintillion calculations per second, each person on the planet would have to be able to crunch about 140 million maths problems in that time. And when quantum computers arrive, they'll be millions of times faster than either of them…

Luckily our survival doesn't depend on us doing maths tests against these astonishing machines. The future isn't a binary, head-to-head, 'us vs them' scenario. We will repeat the leaps we've made before to augment and improve our everyday life.

Our ancestors witnessed a similar process as far back as a million years ago, when they learnt to control fire.[9] It allowed them to stay warm, cook food and fend off animals, setting the scene for Homo sapiens to thrive and make its way to the top of the food chain.

One of the most transformative developments that truly shifted global society was the arrival of man-made electricity in the early 1800s. It's difficult to condense its impact, but it redefined the reality of our planet in an unprecedented way, and no step of progress we've made since its discovery would have been possible without it.

The next evolution of sentient robotics will propel us through another, similar leap. But there will be differences.

Historically, machines have always existed in separation from humans – all tools have, apart from our hands. From the stones we used to crush grain to the remote-controlled robots we use to perform surgery today, there's been a clear definition of where the human ends and the machine begins.

That's set to change, as we perfect machines and technology and integrate them into our bodies. Yes, it sounds creepy, and there's a genuine fear we'll end up like Darth Vader: pseudo-people powered by robotics, immortal until we run out of the energy or money required to upgrade our 'bodies'. But most of us haven't thought about integrated tech in detail. Is it really so different from the glasses and contact lenses that help millions see clearly, or prosthetic limbs that give people a better quality of life?

MAN AND MACHINE

Instead of fearing it, we need to understand how technology can improve our lives.

By 'redesigning' our DNA with the CRISPR-Cas9 tool, we will be able to resist disease and cure hereditary conditions. Using genome editing – technology that allows us to introduce DNA from one strand into another at an exact point – we can augment who we are at the genetic level.[10] Because it mirrors existing DNA behaviour, this process can be used to remove caffeine from coffee beans or allergens from food, and one day we will be able to infuse ourselves with certain traits, store data in our DNA, and halt the ageing process.

And that's just the beginning.

Neural lace is a technology pioneered by one of Elon Musk's lesser known companies, Neuralink. It's an ultra-thin mesh that can be implanted into our brain to ultimately enable the upload of new skills and storage of data. If it sounds familiar, that's because it's basically *The Matrix* (without Agent Smith), and it's part of a bigger move by Neuralink to develop an interface that connects humans and machines.[11]

Neuralink isn't on its own. Uncannily accurate American futurist Ray Kurzweil also predicts the creation of organic-type networks and a synthesis between man and machine.[12]

While it will take some time to connect us to supercomputers, eventually we'll be fused with pseudo-sentient machines and exponentially more intelligent than we are today. And because artificial neural networks mimic the way a human brain operates, we won't be trying to connect organic minds with machines, but rather meeting somewhere in the middle.

The potential of this next human leap is infinite. We are on the brink of unlocking a new humanity, free of disease and armed with answers to problems like poverty, climate change and inequality. This is evolution by technology, and it will be unlike anything we can experience today.

Still, that society will be built on the incremental collective genius we tap into today. We are part of that ongoing 108-billion-strong tribe, laying the groundwork for a generation that will have abundant choice, security and freedom – one that can achieve sci-fi solutions because of the way *we* see the world.

‖‖‖ ‖‖‖

THE BOTTOM LINE

It's exciting to think we may reach this state of singularity by 2045[13], but it also has repercussions we need to consider and prepare for – especially in business. The famous Belgian beer Stella Artois, which was launched in 1926, comes from a brewery with a history that can be traced back to the 1300s. The brewery survived the arrival of electricity, rampant pandemics, the Industrial Revolution and any number of wars on its doorstep because it's in the business of satisfying basic human needs and desires – in this case the need and desire for beer.

It doesn't matter how different our future is from our present; our basic needs and desires will remain, even if they do become more enlightened in time.

So, what will people who live to the age of 200 in a world without disease, with unlimited free energy, where most tasks are handled by AI, want?

Love. Connection. Passion. The unprogrammable, undefinable qualities that make us who we are. No amount of chemical engineering, clever coding or tactile technology will ever remove our fundamental humanity.

20

REDEFINING SUCCESS

THE REVOLUTION IS COMING

It's no secret that innovation and disruption are close to my heart, and often on the tip of my tongue. They're words that have grown into ideas and ultimately become forces of change – markers of our constant progress.

They have also become buzz words and, confusingly, are often used interchangeably. It's important to understand the difference between the two, because each changes our world in a different way.

Innovation is the process that solves problems in new, slightly better ways. It's the app that lets you open and start your car with your phone, or pay for your coffee without a bank card. You're not actually doing anything differently – you're still driving or buying a drink – things are just smoother and easier, and you conserve a small amount of energy for other purposes as a result.

Disruption takes that problem-solving centre and uses it to change the world on a grand scale. The ideas, tools and vision behind companies that render old business models obsolete qualify as truly disruptive. Think what iPods did to music and iPhones to cellphones; what Airbnb is doing to hotels, Netflix streaming content to TV, Instagram to retail, Uber to city transport and Tesla to Uber...

Technology and the exponential future don't care about our history; we all have to be as innovative and disruptive as possible to keep the shop open. Every new idea, from the first flame of a new app to the next big thing in fintech, is leading us forward to a place where innovation and disruption gain the momentum to start a revolution.

THE HUMAN REVOLUTION

Revolution is a loaded gun of a word. It's militant, dangerous even. It makes us think of violence, refusal and resistance. But it also refers to a complete turnaround that points us in a new direction.

The way we think about innovation and disruption is about to undergo a revolution: a human revolution driven by a culture of upliftment that seeks out a better state of wellbeing for everyone.

Those who started the breakaway from the manufacturing mind-set got the wheels turning. As more and more of us start to actively cultivate fluid mind-sets, we see our whole culture starting to turn. In a movement that's gaining momentum, more people and organisations are now embracing peace and seeking positive and ethical impacts. As a result, we're seeing a dramatic shift in the way we see the world.

Please don't get me wrong. Profit is still important. I'm not saying that we should throw out all we've learnt and bank on positive vibes to put food on the table. What I *am* saying is that we're in the midst of a revolution that will see our hunger for immediate 'success' replaced by a more enlightened definition of what success actually means, a long-term approach that prioritises people and our planet over the trappings of the material world.

An example of a company that has clocked the start of that revolution is payment giant Visa. Thanks to its position as the connector between consumers and businesses, it seems unlikely to be disrupted in the next decade, but that hasn't stopped its executives from recognising and reacting to the revolution.

I recently joined Visa at a conference that explored the future of payment, where the company's senior team and leaders chose to engage with fintech start-ups. These are the young guns leading the new way, the inconvenient distractions that many profit-focused listed companies simply ignore or bulldoze out of the way. But the conference saw genuine collaboration, and the sharing of ideas and perspectives for collective gain.

Visa is not yet a revolutionary itself, but it has a sense of the future that sees value in engaging with those who are. I believe it will change its business model sooner rather than later.

This is the way of the future, fuelled by FOREsight, and it's open for all of us to participate in.

DON'T BE A DRAGON

Folklore tells us that, just like leprechauns and Scrooge McDuck, dragons always slept on a pile of gold and jewels.

In some ways, the super-rich elite have tried to do the same, amassing far more wealth than they could spend in their lifetime. Like dragons, they seem to take pleasure from wallowing on a bed of inflated bank balances, spitting fire at any threat. Maybe it's a safety blanket designed to try to make up for the security we've all sacrificed for choice.

When you're trapped in HINDsight, PLAINsight and INsight, this seems like a sound approach. We know we have to make provisions to get through tough times (HINDsight); the more, the better. When we started thinking in an industrial mind-set, we saw in PLAINsight that we could be replaced, just as it made us realise that spectacular wealth was possible in that world. INsight told us we could succeed just by interpreting that information.

When a huge bank balance was a synonym for success, this was all okay. Now, though, in an emotive, human revolution, I believe we're evolving a new perspective. In a time when legacy costings and inherited models are dying away, it seems logical that we use all of that disruptive, innovative thinking for something more profound than simply making money.

Now, being smart with money doesn't mean saving every cent, or haggling every time you buy something to get 'a good deal'. Smart money doesn't sit in a bank, earning cash interest and funding selfish ambition; it gets out there into the real world and gets things done. People who are smart about money are making it non-stop, because they see it as a source of energy. It funds flexibility, rewriting the rule books on wealth.

In the face of this revolution, what matters most is how you can become the best version of yourself, and reflect that value back at humanity through compassion, respect and upliftment. Wealth is measured by our curiosity and our ability to create impact; you certainly don't need to be a billionaire to change the world.

This revolution isn't militant. It's emotional. It wants to leave a legacy of compassion. Tomorrow's leaders will measure their worth by what they do for others, how much they give back and how they are remembered – all of which is the result of applying FOREsight right now to create the future.

|||||||||||||||||||||||||||||||||||||||||||||||||||||||||||||||||| ||||

THE BOTTOM LINE

We're flying towards a future of more, not excess. More personalised moments. More seamless integration and interaction. More affordable goods and services. A future where everything is more intelligent and where we are more human, powered by the fearless pursuit of passion.

I have been called a militant optimist, but I believe that once we become flexible enough to fulfil our freedom and find opportunity everywhere, we'll be able to follow the excitement and forge the future we want.

IN CLOSING

FORGE YOUR FUTURE

We're the luckiest people in human history.

Somehow, we've managed to pop onto the planet at the exact moment when the collective wisdom of generations of geniuses has given us access to technology and innovation that blurs the borders between what we can imagine and what we can create. The fever dreams of sci-fi writers and artists are becoming reality – and we're just getting started.

Of course, not everyone is as optimistic about this world as I am. Our society seems to be split into the daunted and the driven, and the difference is their perspective.

Facing a future full of sentient technology and accelerated change is making a whole lot of people worry – a whole lot. They're worried about their jobs, the future, what the machines will do to us when they rule the world, and a million other things (most of which are well beyond our control).

Sitting on the other side of the table, all smiles and serenity, are those who can stitch together new stories for themselves and their brands; stories that are as compelling and creative as they are elegant.

The difference between these groups is deeper

than their facial expressions. Those who have let go of the perspectives that tie us to the past and root us in the present are excited by the uncertainty of tomorrow; they recognise that it presents boundless opportunities, patterns to be found, invisible dots to be connected into the future they want.

REDEFINE VALUE

There have already been two major shifts that have launched us into a different way of doing things – and they're both linked to what we define as value.

The first was when we started farming. Agricultural society was about subsistence, and our communities depended on the way we worked the land. In that chapter in the human story, value was linked to produce.

That value system got a significant shake-up when we moved from an agricultural to an industrial world. When we swapped farms for factories, we redefined value – and triggered a psychological shift that moved us from valuing produce to valuing what we could produce.

As farmers, we understood ourselves to be the caretakers of nature, nurturing the world in return for food. But when we built machines, we started to think like them. We understood ourselves to be parts of a machine, completing our share of a bigger task and measuring our value by how efficiently we played that part.

The industrial revolution brought with it great advancements, but it geared us to think in a linear, causal way, and to limit our imagination to what we do within a fixed path. That's why most people still equate efficiency with success: we're all processes and project schedules because we still think as if the world is a factory and we're meant to play one small part in the production line.

It's the people who are still locked in that industrial mind-set, where value is linked to efficiency, who can't see the positive potential of society's next shift. To make things worse, they can see people around them leaving that way of thinking behind... but they can't seem to do it.

'It is only with the heart that one can see rightly; what is essential is invisible to the eye.'

ANTOINE DE SAINT-EXUPÉRY,

French writer and poet

FIND FLUIDITY

Just as agricultural society was built on hard work, and the industrial world was all about logistics, our next society is about the new: new ideas, new models, new skills and new definitions.

Never before have we had the tools we have today to explore our world. We have access to endless ideas; the thoughts and discoveries of humanity are a click away. We have the channels and platforms to broadcast and listen to the leading minds of our time. Every moment that passes takes us closer to a new humanity: free of poverty, disease and limitation.

We are perfectly poised to unlearn what we thought we knew and find wisdom. Every moment of every day is a chance to be curious and fully fascinated with our life. And that's the recipe for adaptability.

To lead a great life and leave an unforgettable mark on our collective history, we need to reduce our reliance on the past, accept the limitations of the obvious, and understand that a rich life is lived, not learned.

To peer into the world and pull out patterns that calm chaos and reveal elegance, we need to change our perspective. We can't think like parts of a machine; we have to *be* machines, using the collective genius of those around us to create a new, conscious world.

It's in your hands. You can make an undefinable, unimaginable difference today that becomes a better future for everyone by opening your eyes and imagination to what you want the world to become – and I urge you to do it.

I URGE YOU TO EVOLVE YOUR
PERCEPTION OF WHAT IS POSSIBLE.

I URGE YOU TO STEP OUT OF YOUR
COMFORT ZONE AND LEAP TO PLACES
THAT SCARE YOU.

I URGE YOU TO PREPARE YOUR BODY.
BE FIT. BE HEALTHY. VALUE YOURSELF
IN YOUR ENTIRETY.

I URGE YOU TO CONSCIOUSLY DEVELOP
YOUR OPINIONS. READ, WRITE, CREATE
MEDIA. CONFRONT YOUR TRUTHS,
UNLEARN YOUR PREJUDICES.

I URGE YOU TO CHOOSE PEACE,
NOT VICTORY. COMPASSION IS
OUR MOST PRECIOUS COMMODITY.

I URGE YOU TO BE STEP UP AND INTO
THE BEST VERSION OF YOURSELF, SO
WE CAN CREATE THE BEST VERSION
OF HUMANITY.

I URGE YOU TO SEEK AND CONNECT
THE ELEGANT DOTS BETWEEN PROBLEMS
AND SOLUTIONS.

I URGE YOU TO FORGE YOUR FUTURE
– BECAUSE NOBODY ELSE CAN.

END NOTE

As with my other two books *What's Your Moonshot?* and *Magnetiize*, the information in *FOREsight* has largely been inspired by the many clients, peers and teachers I've interacted with over the years. I have absorbed, adapted, borrowed and refashioned their work in an ongoing process of continuous research, from face-to-face interactions and hearing them talk in person and online, to reading company reports, blogs, articles, websites and more. For this I am hugely grateful – hopefully, I have given back to them in return.

I can't mention every person and publication that has influenced my thoughts, but I believe I have referenced the obvious ones within the text. To those I've no doubt forgotten to mention, I sincerely apologise.

For full references, notes and bibliography, please see the *FOREsight* e-book or visit www.johnsanei.com.

ACKNOWLEDGEMENTS

To the incredible team of people around me – Anita, Kyle, Vince, Lisa, Tim, Ania, Sean and Jenny – thank you for your upward spiral of heartfelt energy and going beyond expectations. And to everyone else who has joined in our journey, thank you. Together, we are building a life of our own design.

in johnsanei

◎ johnsanei

f john.sanei

🐦 IamJohnSanei

🖥 www.johnsanei.com